Spectators on the Paris Stage in the Seventeenth and Eighteenth Centuries

Theater and Dramatic Studies, No. 25

Oscar G. Brockett, Series Editor

Leslie Waggener Professor of Fine Arts
and Professor of Drama
The University of Texas at Austin

Bernard Beckerman, Series Editor, 1980–1983

Brander Matthews Professor of Dramatic Literature
Columbia University in the City of New York

Other Titles in This Series

Spectators on the Paris Stage in the Seventeenth and Eighteenth Centuries

by
Barbara G. Mittman

Associate Professor and Chairperson of French
University of Illinois at Chicago
Chicago, Illinois

PN
2632
M5
1984

UMI RESEARCH PRESS
Ann Arbor, Michigan

Produced and distributed by
UMI Research Press
an imprint of
University Microfilms International
A Xerox Information Resources Company
Ann Arbor, Michigan 48106

Library of Congress Cataloging in Publication Data

Mittman, Barbara G.
  Spectators on the Paris stage in the seventeenth and
eighteenth centuries.

  (Theater and dramatic studies ; no. 25)
  Bibliography: p.
  Includes index.
  1. Theater—France—Paris—History—17th century.
2. Theater—France—Paris—History—18th century.
3. Theater audiences—France—Paris. 4. Theaters—
Stage-setting and scenery. I. Title. II. Series.

PN2632.MB 1984   792'.0944361   84-16339
ISBN 0-8357-1610-4 (alk. paper)

To Joanna Mittman

Contents

List of Figures

Acknowledgments

In the course of preparing this study, I have been aided by a number of individuals who have given generously of their time and of their expertise. I would like first of all to thank Sylvie Chevalley, retired Bibliothécaire-Archiviste of the Comédie Française, who granted me access to the archival material which forms the nucleus of this study, and who took an encouraging interest in my project in its early stages. I would also like to express appreciation to Noëlle Guibert, the current Bibliothécaire-Archiviste, and to her assistant, Jacqueline Razgonnikoff, for their expert and cheerful assistance during my subsequent visits to the Archives of the Comédie Française. Further thanks are owed to Madeleine Jürgens, Conservatrice at the Minutier Central des Notaires de Paris, for her help in identifying and deciphering certain essential documents, and to Nicole Bourdel Felkay, Conservatrice of the Service des plans, cartes et dessins of the Archives Nationales, for advice about iconography.

I would like especially to thank Oscar Brockett for his careful reading of my manuscript, and for the numerous constructive suggestions he offered. I am grateful also to Rémi Clignet, Benjamin Mittman and Robert Mittman for earlier readings. I wish, too, to acknowledge the assistance of George Yanos, Associate Director of the Computing Center at the University of Illinois at Chicago, who patiently helped me conquer the intricacies of that university's word-processing system.

* * *

Permission to adapt previously published articles has been generously granted by *Theatre Research International* and *Theatre Survey*.

Permission to reproduce various illustrations and documents has been granted by the Bibliothèque Nationale, the Bibliothèque de l'Arsenal and the Musée de l'Opéra, as well as by the Minutier Central des Notaires de Paris and the Service des plans, cartes et dessins of the Archives Nationales.

Introduction

How many readers of, say, a Molière play, trying to visualize its performance of 300 years ago, are aware that the stage was occupied not only by actors and actresses, but by dozens and sometimes hundreds of spectators as well? Perhaps not even the history-conscious Ariane Mnouchkine, *auteur* of the fairly recent film *Molière*, was well informed about this practice. Her scene depicting Molière's legendary collapse as he played the *Malade imaginaire* shows none of the twenty-four spectators who, according to the *Registre d'Hubert* for February 17, 1673, were sitting on the stage at that performance.[1]

It is not surprising to find even fairly sophisticated readers of the dramatic literature of seventeenth and eighteenth century France not fully apprised of this custom. Documents shedding light on the subject are few, and historians of the theatre have paid relatively little attention to the matter. However, the presence of petty nobility disporting itself on the stage in tandem with the play in progress was a constant for about 130 years during those two centuries—a constant whose effect was almost always disruptive, and frequently devastating, to the work being performed.

Just how devastating this practice sometimes was is suggested by an anecdote in an eighteenth-century dictionary of the theatre. Typical of many, this anecdote describes the near downfall of the tragedy *Childéric* at its premiere in 1736. During a dramatic high point, a spectator, catching sight of an actor with a letter in his hand trying to make his way through the crowd on the stage, began to shout: "Make way for the mailman!" The outburst of laughter that this provoked "killed the interest of that scene, and very nearly brought the show to a halt."[2]

Because all plays produced in Paris during the last half of the seventeenth century and the first half of the eighteenth century took place against a background of spectators present on the stage, it is essential for students of the theatre of that period to establish as clear a picture as possible of the practice. However, no modern and complete treatment of the subject has yet appeared. The only work entirely devoted to the topic, Adolphe Jullien's thirty-two page monograph, *Le Spectateur sur la scène*, was published in the last century.[3]

Historians of French theatre in our own century have dealt with the spectator on the stage in chapters or sections of works about larger subjects. But each of these treatments is inadequate for one reason or another. Sometimes the matter is considered within the context of *either* the seventeenth century *or* the eighteenth century, instead of as the continuing phenomenon that it was. Elsewhere the approach is anecdotal rather than factual, and significant facts are omitted.

Carelessness or misinterpretation has occasionally led to distortion of the basic picture. The 1966 edition of Castex, Surer and Becker's *Manuel des études littéraires françaises, XVIIe siècle,* for example, proposes that "In 1656, under the influence of England, the rather strange custom was introduced of reserving a certain number of seats or *banquettes* on either side of the stage for the elegant public."[4] There is readily available evidence, however, that the practice was introduced some twenty years before that date, at early performances of the *Cid.* Madame Deierkauf-Holsboer, on the other hand, attempts to push the origins of the practice further back than that play. But, marshaling as evidence an illustration of Rotrou's 1628 *L'Hypocondriaque,* she does not notice that the image in question is clearly from the nineteenth century.[5] A more significant error is put forward by W.L. Wiley in his fine study of the Hôtel de Bourgogne. Stating that "in their new theatre built in 1689 the Comédie Française put in around a dozen rows of banquettes on each side of the stage,"[6] Wiley was probably looking at Adolphe Jullien's erroneous redrawing of the Blondel plan, in which twelve lines replace five rectangles, but whatever the explanation, a total of twenty-four banquettes on the stage of the Comédie Française is a physical impossibility. Additional misrepresentation appears in Peyronnet's study of eighteenth-century stage decoration. Talking, erroneously, about "fixed *banquettes* on the stage ... towards 1637" (movable chairs were still in use until the 1660s), he goes on to say that "until their disappearance in 1759, we know of only TWO series of performances on a cleared stage: one in 1649..., the other...in 1675."[7] The *registres* show repeatedly, however, that spectators were normally banned from the stage for the first run of any major machine play, so many series of performances took place on a cleared stage.

The fact that the problem of spectators on the stage has not as yet been properly treated is no doubt partly a function of the relative paucity of documentary material. The sources of information about this subject, and indeed, about the early history of French public theatres in general, are fairly limited. A brief review of these sources, both documentary and narrative, is in order.

Almost no direct information exists regarding structural aspects of theatres in the first half of the seventeenth century. The only visual documents yet found are two seventeenth-century street maps showing tiny bird's-eye views of the exteriors of the Hôtel de Bourgogne and the Marais Theatre, plus an engraving pertaining to the interior of the Hôtel de Bourgogne.[8] They do not yield satisfactory information about such matters as the size of the stages and the arrangement of audience seating. However, with the help of an important *devis et marché* (proposal and contract) from 1647, scholars have been able to piece together a detailed description of the Hôtel de Bourgogne. In addition, hypothetical elevation/plans of the Marais Theatre based primarily on a 1644 *devis* have been brilliantly rendered by S. Wilma Deierkauf-Holsboer.[9] Thus, despite the lacunae, it has been possible to form some fairly concrete notions of what the Hôtel de Bourgogne and the Marais Theatre must have looked like. As for the Hôtel Guénégaud, the earliest home of the Comédie Française, there is not an iota of structural information.

The story is similar with regard to the public who attended the theatre in France. Not much has survived in the way of written records or *registres* for the early period. As John Lough has pointed out, "neither for the Hôtel de Bourgogne nor for the Marais Theatre . . . do we possess the slightest shred of evidence as to the size of the audience."[10] There is, of course, the precious *Registre de La Grange*,[11] which, in addition to certain information of a circumstantial nature, records the titles of plays and total receipts for each performance of Molière's troupe (eventually merged after his death with other troupes to become the Comédie Française) from Easter 1659 onward to 1685. But La Grange's records, not meant to be a daily account book, do not show how many tickets were sold for the various parts of the theatre. Only three of Molière's daily account books or *registres* have survived. The first two, known as the *Registre de la Thorillière* (they are mostly in the hand of the actor La Thorillière), cover the period from April 1663 to January 1665.[12] But they record expenditures only; receipts were kept in a different *registre,* now lost. The third, called the *Registre d'Hubert,* covers the last year of Molière's career, from April 29, 1672 to March 21, 1673.[13] Because the *Registre d'Hubert* is a daily record of receipts, it yields considerable information about the size and distribution of the audience during that season, including the number of spectators on the stage. No comparable records of any sort exist for the Marais Theatre or the Hôtel de Bourgogne.

There is also, for the seventeenth century, a sometimes astonishing lack of journalistic or narrative record. There are, for instance, no accounts in contemporary gazettes regarding the opening of the Comédie Française in 1689 in its new theatre on the rue des Fossés-Saint-Germain-des-Prés! Not until 1696 on the occasion of the Grand Dauphin's visit to the Comédie Française does the *Mercure Galant* speak of the new theatre.

Matters improve towards the end of the seventeenth century, and in the eighteenth century. A nearly complete set of plans by the architect, François d'Orbay, for the new theatre built by the Comédie Française in 1689 on the rue des Fossés-Saint-Germain-des-Prés are in the Archives of the Comédie Française.[14] In addition, there are the well known Blondel plans, based on the 1689 plans, but modified to represent the Comédie Française in its 1754 state.[15] Revised versions of those appear in the *Encyclopédie* among the plates published in 1772. Another appears in Dumont's 1774 study of French and Italian theatre architecture, and yet another in Roubo's treatise on theatres in 1777.[16] As for the Hôtel de Bourgogne in the eighteenth century, there are two sources of visual information. The first is a set of very rough sketches by an Englishman, Sir James Thornhill, showing plan views and an elevation of the interior of the theatre. (These sketches were discovered not long ago in a diary belonging to the Victoria and Albert Museum in London).[17] The second is the Dumont volume just mentioned, which contains a partial plan showing the Hôtel de Bourgogne as it was in 1773, but from which much information about its earlier state can be extrapolated. Carefully drawn plans for the Palais Royal as it was from 1674, when it became the home of the Opéra, until it burned down in 1763, are preserved in the Archives Nationales.[18]

As for numeric information, all of the *registres* for the Troupe du Roi, which resulted from the merger of the Marais Theatre and the remnants of Molière's troupe after his death, have come down to us. This troupe performed at the Hôtel Guénégaud from 1673 through 1680, and its *registres* (as yet unpublished) are on deposit at the Archives of the Comédie Française.[19] *Registres* for the period starting with formation of the Comédie Française in 1680 to 1774 inclusive have been microfilmed and are on deposit at the Library of Congress.[20] H.C. Lancaster has summarized these records in readily available publications.[21] No account books survive for the Comédie Italienne prior to its banishment from Paris in 1697. However, *registres* for the period starting with its return in 1716 exist and can be consulted at the Bibliothèque de l'Opéra. They are also on microfilm at the Library of Congress.[22]

It should be noted that not all contemporary or near-contemporary information, even when it exists, is necessarily helpful. Indeed, it has been demonstrated that some is quite inaccurate. Lyonnet has shown that the portion of Mouhy's eighteenth-century *Journal manuscrit* which deals with seventeenth-century theatre can be in remarkable error. For example, Mouhy's cast list for the first performance of *Rodogune* at the Hôtel de Bourgogne in 1644 includes four *comédiens* who were either not yet born, or who were only tiny children in 1644.[23] Visual information is not necessarily any more reliable. Eugène Vinaver points out how illustrators who created frontispieces for plays frequently depicted precisely that which could not appear on the stage.[24] In a chapter in *Lieu théâtral,* Lawrenson and Purkis discount the representational accuracy of, among other illustrations, the well-known woodcut depicting a scene from Terence and showing spectators in box seats behind the stage.[25] A much reproduced 1726 engraving after a painting by Coypel showing spectators peeking from behind the curtain of the Comédie Française (see fig. 39) suggests that there is no orchestra between the stage and the *parterre,* whereas all other evidence points to the existence of an orchestra pit at that juncture. Valuable as they are, both verbal and visual sources of information must be regarded with a modicum of skepticism.

Material is limited, then, about the history of seventeenth- and eighteenth-century theatre in general. It is even more limited with respect to the subject of this study. Concrete information about spectators on the stage does not go beyond a few account books, a few engravings and plans, and several documents recently brought to light by this author. Of the *registres* described earlier, only fourteen contain information pertaining specifically to spectators on the stage. These are the *Registre d'Hubert* for the Molière troupe's last season, 1672-73; the *registres* for the Troupe du Roi at the Hôtel Guénégaud, 1673-80; and those for the Comédie Française, 1680-86. During these fourteen seasons, the printed form that was used to record the number of tickets sold called for a separate entry for stage tickets *(billets de théâtre)* (see fig. 1). Starting after the Easter recess of 1686, however, new forms were adopted which abandoned the listing of ticket sales by category of seats in favor of listing ticket sales by price alone. Stage tickets, which fell into the most expensive category, were thus always grouped with the best box seats, such that after 1686 it is no longer possible to ascertain how many were sold.

(It is important to note, before proceeding further, that the word *théâtre* in the seventeenth and eighteenth centuries meant "stage" in the same sense as the words *scène* and *plateau* do today. The entry for "Théâtre" in Furetière's 1690 *Dictionnaire universel* indicates that the term was used to designate not only the building in which the performance took place, or the troupe of actors and actresses, but "also the Stage where the Actors perform." *Billets de théâtre,* then, referred specifically to seats along the sides of the stage.)

Only two plans indicate provisions made for seating spectators on the stage. They are the Thornhill sketches mentioned above of the Hôtel de Bourgogne during the Regency, and the mid-eighteenth-century plan of the Comédie Française which appears in Blondel. Some fifteen illustrations of various types (engravings, drawings, fan decorations) dating from the middle seventeenth century to the middle eighteenth century and beyond, depict spectators on the stage. In addition, five newly published documents having to do with the installation of the balustrade at the Ancienne Comédie also contribute information about stage seating.[26]

There is also informative, if sporadic, reportage about spectators on the stage in gazettes or private journals. The most specific and useful of these sources is Barbier's *Journal.*[27] Anecdotes in early dictionaries and histories of the theatre also make their contribution, as do references in private correspondence. Additionally, there are innumerable descriptions of the

Aujourd'huy mardy 14ᵉ jour de Feburier 1673

Au Malade Imaginaire

Theatre trente deux billets 176ᵗᵗ

Loges Sept loges et trente six billets . . . - 506ᵗᵗ

Amphi-Theatre quatre vingtz cinq billets . . 467ᵗᵗ 10ʃ

Loges hautes cent trente th billets 393ᵗᵗ

Loges du 3ᵉ rang Vnze billets 22ᵗᵗ

Parterre a 3ᵗ deux cens dix billets 315ᵗᵗ

Receu en tout 1879ᵗᵗ 10ʃ

Frais ordinaires et extraordinairs 268ᵗᵗ 5ʃ

Gardes a Vn garçon qui a averty les danceurs 3ᵗᵗ

Feu et menus frais a Crosnier 4ᵗᵗ 10ʃ

Menus frais de la porte 1ᵗᵗ 15ʃ

Afsistans Rendu a Mʳ Baraillon pour Vn habit rebrir
de Mʳ Moliere . . . . _ _ _ _ 22ᵗᵗ

Frais extraordinaires

PART 80ᵗᵗ

Reste és mains de Monsieur Hubert Trois cens liures pour
10 frais .

Retiré par Monsieur

Figure 1.   Page of Daily *Registre* Before 1686

custom in literature of the period. Perforce constructed for maximum effect, these descriptions and accounts are almost certainly exaggerated. By the same token, they surely communicate the flavor and atmosphere of that curious custom better than any account book, plan or notarized document.

The study which follows puts together all of the information currently available on the subject to present as clear and comprehensive a picture as possible of the practice of seating spectators on the stage in the seventeenth and eighteenth centuries in public theatres in Paris.

1

The Development of Stage Seating in the Early Years

Knowledge about the development of stage seating in Paris theatres in the early years, that is, prior to the formation of the Comédie Française in 1680, has to be deduced from very little. Only a handful of engravings, a few scattered remarks in chronicles and elsewhere and the *Registre d'Hubert* for 1672-73 offer relevant information. Nevertheless, it is possible to weave a fairly satisfying account of the evolution of stage seating during its earliest decades.

There probably was not a clear-cut beginning of the practice of admitting spectators to the stage. Outdoor theatres in the Middle Ages had consisted of one or more scaffolds raised several feet off the ground, perhaps arranged in a rough circle. Actors occupied these scaffolds at the start of a performance, but could also descend to the ground, where the audience stood. In some cases, scaffolds were also used to accommodate sections of the audience.[1] Later, nostrum peddlars gathered spectators on three sides of the stage and encouraged them to mount up on the stage to effect a purchase.[2] Thus, historically, there was not a formalized separation between performers and the public. As theatre troupes began performing in unused indoor tennis courts *(jeux de paume)* in Paris in the late sixteenth century, there was doubtless a continuation of the informal relationship between audience and actors characteristic of medieval theatre. Actors not engaged in playing a scene sometimes came to sit on either side at the front of the stage, where they remained in view of the spectators throughout the play.[3] Spectators, particularly pages and lackeys, occupied nooks and crannies of the board-and-trestle stages (see fig. 2).[4]

Theatre life in Paris remained transient and sporadic through the early decades of the seventeenth century. Although Paris already had one permanent theatre building, the Hôtel de Bourgogne, the city did not acquire a permanent theatre troupe until nearly 1630. Before that, the Confrérie de la Passion, owners of the Hôtel de Bourgogne, rented its theatre to itinerant troupes from the provinces and from abroad. The new resident company, which enjoyed protected status, was designated as the Troupe Royale. It was joined before

Figure 2.   Frontispiece. *Les Fantaisies
de Bruscambille
(Bibliothèque Nationale)*

long by a second resident company, which installed itself in 1634 in the Théâtre du Marais in the Rue Vieille du Temple.

The ground floor, or *parterre*, of the Hôtel de Bourgogne and the Marais Theatre did not contain fixed seating, except for resting benches along the side walls underneath the galleries. Spectators stood or milled about during the spectacle, just as they were accustomed to doing outdoors. Also reminiscent of outdoor habit was the presence of concessionaires peddling beverages and snacks in the *parterre*. For a time, very early in the century, stools and portable benches were permitted in the pit, but by 1622 the Hôtel de Bourgogne no longer allowed them, and the *parterre* was completely given over to standees.[5]

The type of spectator to be found on the stage in the first decades of the seventeenth century was a far cry from the powdered and beribboned dandy that populated stages later in the century. Indeed, theatre audiences as a whole were a different breed. Theatres were patronized mainly, but not exclusively, by rowdies and unsavory characters, while women by and large stayed away.[6] Attracted by *farceurs* such as Bruscambille and Turlupin, those who did venture to the theatre saw slapstick routines featuring characters with interminable beards and baggy pants, or heard comic discourses with titles such as "Facetious Prologue on the Usefulness of the Posterior," or "Preamble on Tits."[7] However, in the 1630s and 1640s, as polite society developed in the salons, both Paris theatres began making an effort to attract a better class of clientele. Repertories were upgraded, the auditoriums were redecorated, and more *loges* were installed, thereby reducing the amount of space for noisy standees.[8] By 1636, Guez de Balzac considered that Paris theatres had been "cleansed of all sorts of trash," such that respectable people of refinement and social standing could attend.[9] It seems likely that before this took place, the stage was occupied primarily by pages, lackeys and an occasional author, all admitted free.

It was doubtless not until 1637, when the monumentally successful *Cid* created seating pressures at the Marais Theatre, that viewing plays from the stage became a status symbol among the nobility. Montdory, actor and head of the Troupe du Marais, describes how this took place.

> The crowd at our doors was so large and our premises so small, that the recesses along the sides of the stage, occupied by pages on other occasions, became preferred seating for Chevaliers du Saint-Esprit, and there were ordinarily wearers of the Cordon Bleu gracing the stage.[10]

The nooks and recesses formed by the compartmentalized stage decor, or *mansions,* still used for early performances of the *Cid* had thus been turned into privileged seating for titled gentlemen.

Such an abrupt conversion was not accomplished without friction, however, for the pages and lackeys who had been in the habit of occupying these spaces were not easily dispossessed of their territory. Some commentary on a play first given about 1640 reveals the tensions created as former occupants of the stage sill attempted to take their places there. Critical of the way in which D'Aubignac's *La Pucelle d'Orléans* was being performed, the commentator would have preferred "a dozen actors on the stage to portray the feelings of the soldiers against the Council when the verdict was handed down." Instead, there were "only two guards, who seemed to be on the stage more to prevent pages and lackeys from getting up there, than to participate in the portrayal of such a notable moment in history."[11]

Despite such friction, the seating of nobility on the stage seems to have become a well established practice fairly quickly, at Paris's main theatre, the Marais, if perhaps not yet at the Hôtel de Bourgogne. The exception was performances of machine plays, whose complicated mechanical works occupied most of the space at the sides of the stage, and prevented the accommodation of spectators there. Rotrou, in his libretto for the *Naissance d'Hercule,* performed at the Marais in 1649, remarks that "It is an advantage that machine plays chase courtiers from the stage."[12] It is thus established that little more than a decade after the overflow crowd at the *Cid,,* aristocratic spectators, though absent from the stage of the Marais during machine plays, were normally present there at other times.

There is some likelihood, on the other hand, that the Hôtel de Bourgogne did not make a regular practice of seating aristocracy on the stage until after its remodeling in 1647. Scarron, in a work published in 1648 but doubtless describing the theatre in its earlier state, observes that "the Hôtel de Bourgogne is swarming with [authors] all the way up onto the stage, because they don't pay anything, the same as the pages."[13] It is not clear whether authors, admitted free, rubbed elbows on the stage with nobility or with domestics, but it is known that the Hôtel de Bourgogne was somewhat behind the Marais in attracting high-quality clientele. After the theatre occupied by the Marais troupe was rebuilt in 1644 as a consequence of a disastrous fire, it had forty boxes suitable for gentlemen and their ladies, while the Hôtel de Bourgogne had only twelve, of which eight were reserved for the Maîtres de la Confrérie who owned the premises. But after its remodeling in 1647, the Hôtel de Bourgogne was once again in a competitive position, having installed some 300 box seats (about the same number as the Marais) with which to attract upper-crust Parisian society.[14] Modifications were also made in the stage area: actors' *loges* (dressing rooms) surrounding the stage were removed, thereby creating space at the sides of the stage for storage and deployment of decorations. It is almost certain that if courtiers were not already a regular feature of the Hôtel de Bourgogne stage, they became so at that point.

In any event, the practice of seating gentlemen on the stage was firmly established in both theatres by 1657, when the chronicler Tallemant des Réaux writes:

> At the present time there is a frightful inconvenience at the Comédie, in that both sides of the stage are quite full of young men seated on straw-bottomed chairs. This is because they do not wish to be in the *parterre*, even though soldiers are often stationed at the door, and neither pages nor lackeys carry swords any more. Box seats are quite expensive, and one must think of them ahead of time; for an *écu* or for half a louis one can be on the stage; but that spoils it all, and all it takes is one insolent fellow to upset everything.[15]

Tallemant's complaint confirms that pages and lackeys no longer sat on the stage but had been relegated to the *parterre*.

Tallemant also reveals that seating facilities on the stage had evolved. The young courtiers who now occupied the stage sat on straw-bottomed chairs, and not in the niches mentioned in Montdory's letter of twenty years earlier. It is also noteworthy that in 1657 seats on the stage were less expensive and easier to obtain than seats in the boxes. A 1662 engraving illustrating Poisson's *Zig-Zag*, a one-act comedy played at the Hôtel de Bourgogne, gives an idea of how spectators on the stage looked at that juncture (see fig. 3).

Molière, upon his return to Paris in 1658, seems promptly to have adopted this practice. The stage of the Petit Bourbon, where Molière's troupe first performed, was well populated with "persons of rank,"[16] as was, presumably, that of the Palais Royal, which became Molière's home theatre starting in 1660.[17] Molière no doubt welcomed the income from these seats as much as anyone else, willingly trading esthetics for revenue. But he did not for that reason spare the occupants of these stage seats from periodic ridicule: *Les Fâcheux* (1661), *La Critique de l'Ecole des femmes* (1663) and the *Misanthrope* (1666) all contain passages satirizing these "fashionable people" who posed and pranced about the stage hoping to cut an intellectual figure, but who only succeeded in creating "a row at all the best moments."[18] (Such language notwithstanding, Molière himself seems to have been a spectator on the stage at least once, at the rival Hôtel de Bourgogne where in 1663 he watched Boursault's *Le Portrait du peintre, ou la contre-critique de l'Ecole des femmes.)*[19]

As we have seen, stage seating had progressed from available space in the recesses mentioned by Montdory in 1637 to the use of the movable chairs indicated by Tallemant twenty years later. Chairs are referred to again in 1661, as one of Molière's *fâcheux* views a play from the front of the stage, where "he planted his chair" (I,i). Chairs can also be seen in the 1662 *Zig-Zag* engraving (fig. 3).[20] With arms and upholstered seats, they appear more elaborate than the simple straw-bottomed ones mentioned by Tallemant.

Figure 3.   Frontispiece, *Le Zig-Zag*
Hôtel de Bourgogne, 1662
(Bibliothèque de l'Arsenal)

In the mid-1660s, however, all three Paris theatres eliminated movable chairs in favor of less disruptive benches. We can presume that the Marais Theatre had acquired benches by 1663 because a character in a play whose setting is the stage of that same theatre complains that the stage benches are uncomfortable and demands a chair.[21] Benches existed at the Hôtel de Bourgogne by 1666, as evidenced by an engraving illustrating Brécourt's *Noce de village* (fig. 4). The Palais Royal must have had benches by 1666 as well, for in the *Misanthrope* Acaste boasts of having sat "on the stage benches" (III.i). Despite complaints about their discomfort, stage benches apparently received thorough use, because by 1671, according to La Grange's *Registre,* those at the Palais Royal were already in need of refurbishing.[22]

There is no direct information describing the size or arrangement of these benches. It is known, however, that Molière held the number of seats to thirty-two (see chapter 4), so it is likely that the Palais Royal had, at either side of the stage, two benches accommodating eight spectators each. (Molière's thirty-two spectators could not have been strung out into single rows of sixteen, for that arrangement would have blocked too many wings.) On the other hand, at the Hôtel de Bourgogne, judging from the 1666 engraving referred to above, there was only one row of benches at each side of the stage, probably intended to seat eight or ten, with standees behind. No such clues exist for the Marais Theatre, but it is not likely that practice differed greatly among Paris theatres. In any case, at popular performances, the seating capacity on stage was increased by the addition of several chairs (see fig. 5).

The changeover from chairs to benches may have immobilized the seats on stage, but did not immobilize the "fashionable people" who occupied them. Heedless of the official performance taking place center stage, this segment of the audience put on its own performance, coming and going at random, making entrances and exits right along with the players. Writing in 1668, the Abbé de Pure ruefully describes this state of affairs:

> The stage should be kept empty, except for actors. The people who are on it, or who arrive on it during the performance, cause intolerable disorder and confusion. How often, on hearing bits of verse such as: "But here he is, I see him," has one taken for an actor, for the expected character, some good-looking, well-dressed gentleman entering the stage and looking for a seat, even after several scenes have already been played.[23]

The deliberateness with which the *petits marquis* carried on is evoked in lively (if exaggerated) fashion by a passage in Campistron's *L'Amante amant* (1684). One of the comedy's characters, a nobleman, describes how he and his friends behaved.

Figure 4.   Scene, *La Noce de village*
            Hôtel de Bourgogne, 1666
            (Bibliothèque Nationale, Cabinet des Estampes)

Figure 5.   Scene, *La Noce de village*
             Hôtel de Bourgogne, 1666
             (Bibliothèque Nationale, Cabinet des Estampes)

We take our seats on the stage, three or four of us on each side, at some distance from one another. We chat; we take snuff; we use our handkerchiefs often; we cross from one side of the stage to the other; we come back to our original seat; and at the most moving moments we play a little prank or crack a joke, good or bad, it matters not. We laugh immediately. Half the *parterre* laughs too; the other half is enraged. All that together creates a lot of noise. The actor stops; he becomes discouraged; his momentum is lost; his acting is no longer worth anything; there's the play gone to the devil.[24]

Not everyone agreed that the *petits marquis* were all bad. Chappuzeau, acknowledging the impediment they created, but perhaps sensing theatre's destiny as more of a social phenomenon than an artistic one, considered the *petits marquis* an asset. "The actors often have great difficulty making their entrances onto the stage," he observed in 1673, "because the wings are so full of gentlemen of quality, who perforce ornament it richly."[25]

In any case, it is against such a disruptive backdrop that all plays given at the time must be imagined. *Andromaque* at the Hôtel de Bourgogne, *Cinna* at the Marais, *Tartuffe* at the Palais Royal—none was immune. Hermione emoted and Auguste deliberated amidst a flock of *petits marquis;* and Tartuffe, looking about to see if "anyone might surprise him seducing his friend's wife," is surrounded by "a hundred witnesses of his tête-à-tête with her."[26] Already intolerable, the situation was to grow much worse over the next decades.

Stage Seating at the Ancienne Comédie and the Other Paris Theatres

After the death of Molière in 1673, the remnants of his troupe were merged with the Marais troupe. Known as the Troupe du Roi, they moved over to the Hôtel Guénégaud (Lully having preempted the Palais Royal for his Opéra), and were keenly competitive with the Hôtel de Bourgogne. In 1680, by royal decree, an amalgamation of the Troupe du Roi and the Hôtel de Bourgogne troupe created the Comédie Française. The newly chartered company, which performed at the Hôtel Guénégaud, was granted a monopoly on the performance of French tragedy and comedy in Paris and its environs. Besides the Comédie Française, Paris continued to support two other official theatres, the Comédie Italienne and the Opéra. Italian players had been on the Paris scene off and on since the sixteenth century, were eventually promoted to official status as the Comédie Italienne, and performed Italian material at the Hôtel de Bourgogne until their twenty-year banishment which began in 1697. The Opéra continued to offer lyrical spectacle at the Palais-Royal. In addition, the two large seasonal fairs, the Foire Saint Laurent and the Foire Saint Germain had theatres connected with them. All of these organizations had to contend with the problem of spectators on the stage.

The Ancienne Comédie

In 1689, the Comédie Française was permitted to purchase and move into new quarters on the rue des Fossés-Saint-Germain-des-Prés (today rue de l'Ancienne Comédie). The premises acquired by the troupe consisted of an old *jeu de paume* and two adjacent buildings suitable for conversion to a theatre. The Comédie Française occupied that theatre, later known as the Ancienne Comédie, for the next eighty-three years. Although the troupe received a certain amount of financial assistance from the king and was directly under the king's authority, for a number of years the actors and actresses enjoyed administrative and artistic autonomy. Later, as Louis XIV declined, the

Gentlemen of the King's Bed Chamber intervened more and more frequently and capriciously in the affairs of the Comédie Française, often dictating the assignment of choice roles and which plays were to be given.

By the end of the seventeenth century, the practice of closing for three weeks during the Easter season had become firmly established. Apart from obligatory closings on a few other religious holidays, performances at the Comédie Française were scheduled on a daily basis throughout the year, including Sundays. However, performances during the summer months, when fashionable people were out of town, were generally poorly attended, and closings because of extreme heat or because "nobody came" were not unusual.[1] Until the latter part of the seventeenth century, theatre performances in Paris started at two or three o'clock in the afternoon, but by the time the Comédie Française moved to the rue des Fossés-Saint-Germain-des-Prés, starting times had been moved back to five o'clock or later.[2] The Comédie Française scheduled either one long play alone, or a long play and a one-act comedy together. There was always a musical interval or intermission between acts. This allowed time for the trimming of wicks on the multitudinous candles used to light the stage and the auditorium, which remained illuminated throughout the play.[3]

The general configuration of the new Comédie Française auditorium was not unlike that of its predecessors (the Hôtel Guénégaud, the Hôtel de Bourgogne and the Marais Theatre), except for the important fact that it was U-shaped rather than rectangular in form. No doubt looking to what Lulli had done with the Opéra auditorium when the Palais Royal was remodeled in 1674, François d'Orbay, the architect hired by the troupe, broke away somewhat from the old tennis court shape by rounding the back of the theatre.[4] As in the older theatres, the ground floor of the auditorium had a large *parterre* for standees. To the rear, a graduated amphitheatre held fixed benches, while to the front, between the *parterre* and the stage, was an area designated as the *orchestre*. The *orchestre* had seating for the theatre's dozen or so musicians and, if not at the outset, soon thereafter, additional seating reserved for Gentlemen of the King's Bed Chamber. Running around the U-shape of the auditorium were three rows of boxes *(loges)*, which extended onto the stage. The boxes on the stage were situated behind the curtain and were known as *balcons*. There were two tiers of *balcons* on either side of the stage, in the space between the front edge of the stage and the first wing flat.

From all indications, the practice of seating spectators on the stage at the Ancienne Comédie continued, at least initially, about as it had been at the three predecessor theatres. Permanent seating consisted of two rows of *gradins* (tiered benches) on either side of the stage, in front of the *balcons*. As before, this seating was intended to accommodate a relatively modest number of gentlemen. The new theatre, however, incorporated a feature that had probably not existed at the earlier theatres, namely a wrought iron balustrade forming an enclosure around the stage benches.

The general appearance of these enclosures, called *enceintes de la balustrade*, is shown in a 1690 engraving by Le Pautre illustrating Boursault's very successful *Fables d'Esope* (fig. 6). A fairly precise description of the area can be constructed with the aid of several documents only recently brought to light by the author. The most informative of these documents are a special account book kept by La Grange detailing expenditures for the new theatre and a very detailed contract between the Comédie Française and an iron-worker for installation of the balustrade. Consisting of about a dozen gilded wrought iron panels approximately two feet wide by three feet high, capped by as many golden pommels, the balustrade started at each downstage corner and curved around sufficiently to enclose the two rows of *gradins*.[5] Then, running parallel to the stage boxes, it continued towards the back of the stage. Each balustrade was four and one-quarter *toises* (8.28 meters) in length and extended upstage to about the level of the third wing flat. Of the six wing openings in that theatre, the first two were thus effectively inactivated for stage production purposes (see figs. 7 and 8). Green melton fabric *(drap vert)* covered the floor boards inside the enclosure, perhaps to cut down on the noise of shuffling feet. The same green fabric, of which over forty yards in all were purchased, covered the seats of the two rows of tiered benches.

Later, probably during the Régence, stage seating at the Comédie Française was greatly expanded. Two short rows of tiered benches on each side of the stage became four and one-half long rows. The wrought iron balustrade was accordingly expanded and lengthened, and the *enceinte de la balustrade* took up more room than ever. The way the stage was ultimately laid out is shown by the plan published in Blondel's 1754 *Architecture Française* (fig. 9). The details of this increase in stage seating are discussed in chapter 4.

Access to the stage seats at the Ancienne Comédie was via the *foyers* or greenrooms adjacent to the queen's side of the stage (the left as one faces the stage). From there, a wide door and four steps led down into the wing area, which in turn afforded access to the *gradins* (see figs. 9 and 10). Spectators holding king's side tickets were obliged to traverse the stage in order to reach their seats, since entry on the king's side appears to have been blocked by unused scenery. (According to the legend for the Blondel plan, "the area marked (&) [see fig. 9] is intended for storage of decorations that are used only occasionally.") Latecomers to the king's side, of course, caused maximum disruption. Crossing the stage while the play was in progress, they were readily mistaken for actors making an entrance. During intermissions, the *petits marquis* seated on the stage had no choice but to repair to the *foyers* to mingle, which was, needless to say, one of the reasons they had come in the first place.

Figure 6.   Frontispiece. *Les Fables d'Esope*
Comédie Française, 1690
(Bibliothèque Nationale)

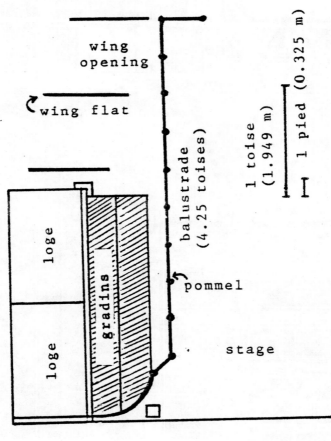

wing
opening

wing flat

loge

loge

gradins

balustrade
(4.25 toises)

pommel

stage

1 toise
(1.949 m)

1 pied (0.325 m)

auditorium

Figure 7. Hypothetical Diagram, Balustrade Area, Comédie
Française

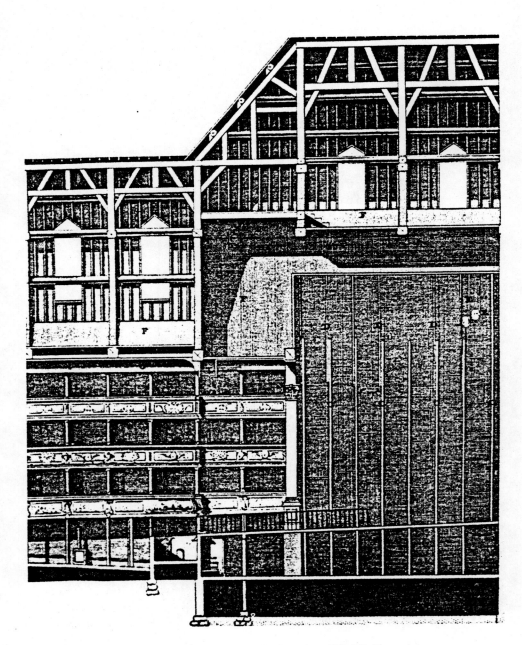

Figure 8.   Detail, Longitudinal Elevation, Comédie Française
(Blondel, *Architecture Française*)

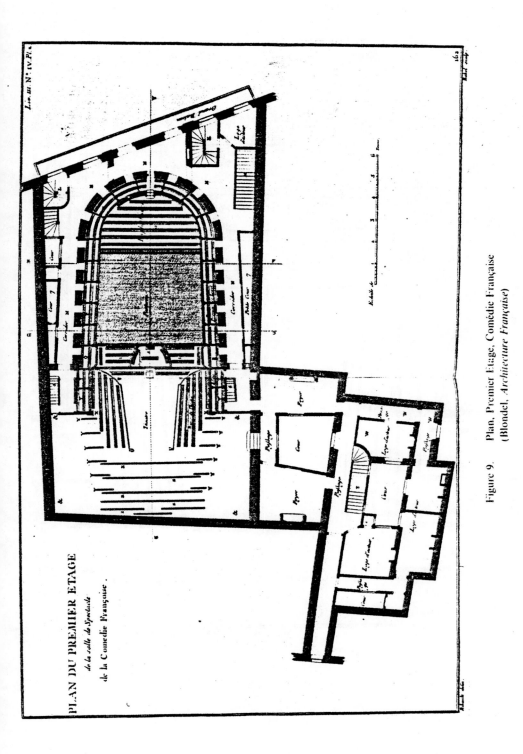

Figure 9.   Plan, Premier Étage, Comédie Française
(Blondel, *Architecture Française*)

Figure 10.   Detail, Premier Etage, Comédie Française
             (Blondel, *Architecture Française*)

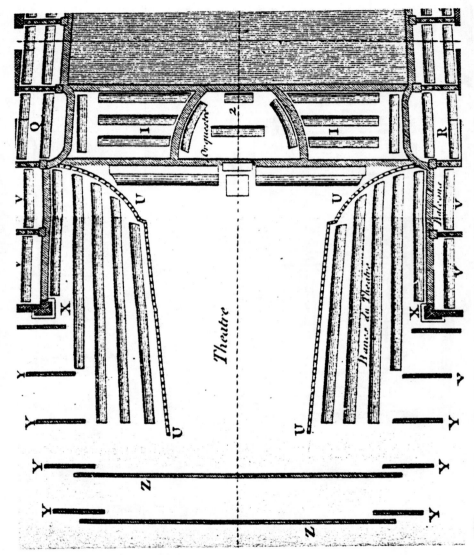

The Other Theatres

The Comédie Française, of course, was hardly alone in facing the problem of spectators on the stage. The two other year-round public theatres, that is the Opéra and the Comédie Italienne, also at one time or another permitted spectators to view the play from the stage, as did the theatres connected with the two large seasonal fairs, the Foire Saint Laurent and the Foire Saint Germain.

Although the Opéra initially resisted this practice, by the 1680s if not before, it too had succumbed. Du Tralage, a contemporary observer of the theatre, relates how, despite Lully's opposition, this lucrative custom finally became established at the Opéra.

> In the past Mr. Lully was very touchy on that point, and no one went to the orchestra or to the stage, except for actors and musicians. However, when the Dauphin attended the Opéra, his too-numerous entourage, as well as the courtiers who came to be seen ... were placed, for want of other space, wherever there was room [i.e., on the stage], and what started as an inconsequential accident ended up becoming a habit.[6]

Du Tralage further reports that for thirty or forty *pistolles* one could become a subscriber and attend the Opéra as often as one wished. Subscribers could "choose whatever seating they desired, ordinarily the stage on account of *les filles.*"[7]

Lully, thinking to diminish the appeal of stage seats, "doubled the price of these seats to one gold louis," thereby rendering them twice as expensive as the far better seats in the boxes and the amphitheatre. But unfortunately this tactic only made them more sought after, causing "these gentlemen to become more desirous of being there, in order to be seen, as well as for the pleasure of making sweet talk to the actresses most to their liking."[8]

The popularity of this practice at the Opéra is confirmed by a passage from Dufresny's *Amusements sérieux et comiques,* a 1699 forerunner of the *Lettres persanes.* The narrator is taking a visitor from Siam to the Opéra for the first times.

> 'Let us enter quickly, then, and take seats on the stage.' 'On the stage,' replied my Siamese, 'you're joking! It is not we who are the entertainment: we're here to see it.' 'No matter,' I told him, 'let's go show ourselves there: one doesn't see a thing, one hears badly; but that's the most expensive spot, and consequently the most honorable. However, since you're not yet in the habit of the Opéra, being on the stage won't give you the kind of pleasure that makes up for the loss of the show. Follow me to a box; while waiting for the curtain to go up, I'll tell you a bit about what is behind it.'[9]

An impediment at straight dramatic performances, the presence of spectators on the stage of the Opéra, with its machinery and elaborate stage sets, must have been a veritable nightmare.

The Comédie Italienne, following the lead of the Comédie Française and its predecessor theatres, permitted spectators on the stage both before and after its banishment from Paris. (The Italian players, it will be recalled, were forced to absent themselves from Paris for nearly twenty years, from 1697 to 1716, after having allegedly satirized Mme de Maintenon in *La Fausse Prude.*) Sharing first the Palais Royal with Molière's troupe (1660-1673), and subsequently the Hôtel Guénégaud with the Troupe du Roi (1673-1680), the Comédie Italienne could hardly have avoided stage seating.[10] After their move to the Hôtel de Bourgogne in 1680 and until their expulsion seventeen years later, they continued to place spectators on the stage. Du Tralage indicates the price of a stage seat there in 1688 (one *écu*)[11] and in Regnard's *La Coquette,* performed by the Comédie Italienne in 1691, there is reference to "a foppish fellow who plants himself . . . on the stage benches." Asked why he does not view the play from a box where he might enjoy privacy, the courtier retorts:

> I in a box? Ha! I beg your pardon. I don't listen to a play from a box like a little bird; by golly, I want to be seen from head to toe; the only reason I spend my *écu* is so that I can circulate during the intermissions and flit about among the actresses.[12]

Upon the return of the Comédie Italienne to Paris in 1716 (the theatre-loving Régence had lost little time in restoring its royal privilege), spectators once again took their places on the stage of the Hôtel de Bourgogne, which had remained empty during the Italian troupe's exile. The ordinance permitting "the re-establishment of a new company of Italian actors" takes particular note of this group of spectators. In standard ordinance language, they are expressly forbidden from stopping "in the wings which serve as entry-ways to the stage . . . and outside the area enclosed by the balustrades put there in order to keep the spectators seated behind them and separated from the actors.[13]

Not surprisingly, the seasonal Théâtres de la Foire joined the year-round theatres in welcoming spectators to the stage. A March 15, 1710 police report regarding the Foire Saint Germain states that there was "such a great quantity of men standing that the stage was nearly covered with them, barely leaving a tiny space for the actors, which was the reason that once in a while someone cried aloud: *Make room on the stage!*"[14] An additional police report indicates that the largest and best appointed of the fair theatres, opened in 1711 by the Chevalier Pellegrin, had seating on the stage. It consisted of, on either side of the stage, three rows of stalls with upholstered benches closed at each end by iron balustrades.[15]

Given the casual type of material that was usually offered at the fair theatres, the presence of spectators on the stage was probably less detrimental than at the regular theatres, and could sometimes even be advantageously incorporated in the play itself. The second act of D'Orneval's *Arlequin traitant* (1716), for instance, calls for an incident involving a supposed spectator seated on a stage bench. Heckled by Arlequin, the spectator becomes angry and attacks the actors. "The guard arrives on the stage, which leaves the spectators expecting a serious event; but the man, who happens to be an actor, begins to sing. . . . He is interrupted by cries of surprise from the spectators, who happily recognize their mistake."[16]

Certainly the informal atmosphere that prevailed at these theatres must have been particularly conducive to stage seating. However, at least some of the time it was declared against the rules for spectators to be there. A royal ordinance concerning the theatres at the Saint Laurent and Saint Germain fairs which was promulgated on January 17, 1726 and again on January 15, 1742 forbids "all persons, whatever their rank or station . . . to position themselves on the stage."[17] In any case, numerous royal ordinances promulgated throughout the first half of the eighteenth century, and meant to regulate the practice, attest to its continuing existence at both Théâtres de la Foire.[18] Ordinances notwithstanding, matters sometimes simply got out of control there. At the closing performance of Favart's *Acajou* at the Foire Saint Germain in 1744, so many spectators jammed the stage that "only one actor at a time could appear on it."[19]

Spectators also sat on the stage in private theatres. An illustration of a 1745 performance of Voltaire and Rameau's *Princesse de Navarre* at the Palais de Versailles shows a small draped enclosure at each side of the stage, within which are seated a small number of spectators (fig. 26). Provision for spectators on the stage can also be seen in a plan of a small public theatre built in Versailles in 1756. This plan (fig. 11) shows a *banquette* in front of each stage box. Measuring by the scale which appears on the plan, the benches were about nine *pieds* in length, hence roomy enough to accommodate six spectators apiece.[20] In addition, spectators are shown on the stage in two illustrations depicting a children's theatre. These little illustrations, which decorate two fans (figs. 12 and 13), show a dozen or so gentlemen seated behind wrought iron balustrades in front of the stage boxes. The practice was apparently also adopted at an early date in the provinces. According to a contemporary witness at a tragedy performed at the Collège de Clermont on August 22, 1662, there were spectators, both men and boys, present on the stage.[21]

As we have seen, the custom in Paris of allowing spectators to view a play from the vantage point of the stage evolved within a relatively short time from a casual, informal practice to a formal and highly developed one. Where initially a few pages and lackeys might slip unobtrusively into the niches between the compartments or *mansions* of a simultaneous décor, by the middle of the seventeenth century stage seating had become established and fashionable—a full-scale operation involving, at the Comédie Française, fixed seating for dozens and eventually hundreds of gentlemen. The practice flourished in both public and private theatres, in Paris and in the provinces for well over a century.

The next chapter will examine some of the psychology related to the popularity of this intrusive custom.

Figure II.   Plan, Public Theatre at Versailles, 1756
            (Dumont, *Parallèle des plans*)

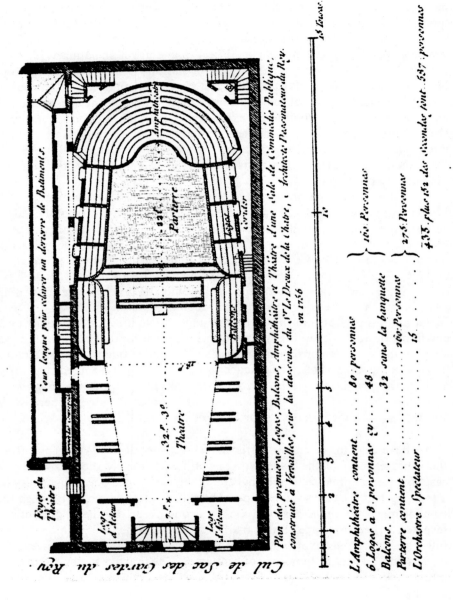

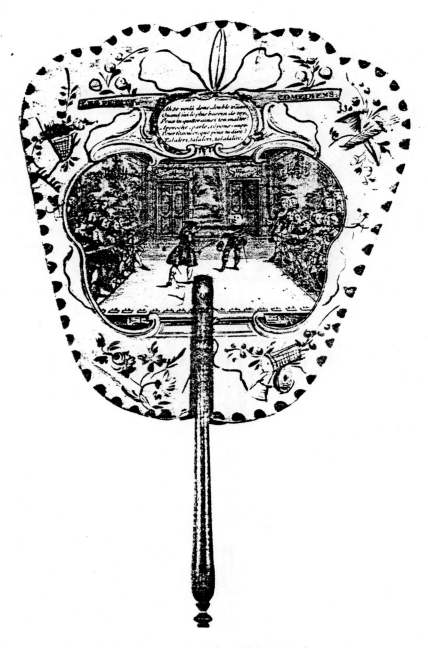

Figure 12.   Fan Depicting Les Petits Comédiens
            (Musée de l'Opéra)

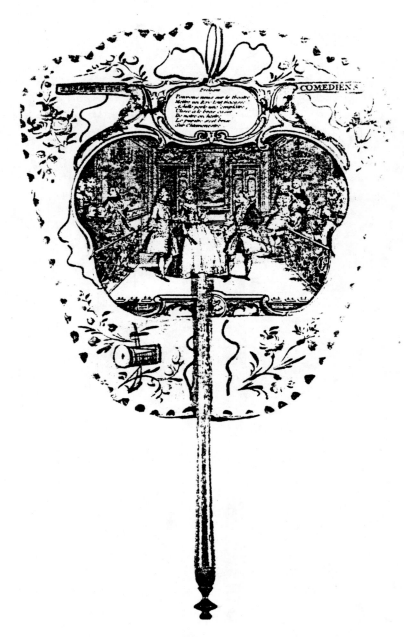

Figure 13. Fan Depicting Les Petits Comédiens
(Musée de l'Opéra)

3

Some Social and Aesthetic Considerations

Once discovered, the notion of stage seating as a desirable activity caught on quickly and lasted a long time. Yet stage seating not only interfered seriously with the conduct of the play, but provided the spectators who used it with the poorest of vantage points. Objectively, the practice was unsatisfactory from every view save that of troupe members counting the extra gold *louis* brought in by the seats on the stage. However, less objective factors were also at work. The most important had to do with the social behavior and motivations of the petty aristocracy who populated the stage, and for whom attendance at the theatre was a significant means of self-expression. In addition, certain aesthetic factors related to the baroque were probably of consequence in prolonging the presence of spectators on the Paris stage.

Social Motivations

At all of the Paris theatres, viewing a play from the stage had evolved as a male prerogative. Women did not normally venture onto the stage, although they did, of course, sit in the *loges de balcon* or stage boxes after these were installed in the 1670s. The stage seats proper were occupied by men alone. A charming seventeenth-century drawing (fig. 14) depicting spectators on the stage of an unidentified theatre illustrates the distribution of that population.[1] Men only are seated on the three-tiered benches *(gradins)* giving directly onto the stage. In the two boxes above, there is a mixture of gentlemen and ladies.

Before the end of the century, stage seats became associated primarily with a group of dandies referred to as *petits marquis* or, as they eventually came to be known, *petits-maîtres*. The latter term appears to have come into use towards 1683 to designate a little band of young nobles dedicated to leading life in as outrageous and shocking a manner possible. Dressed in extreme or affected clothing, these young men were later described by Voltaire as "white-

Figure 14.   Drawing, Seventeenth-Century Stage Spectators
(Archives Nationales, Service des plans, cartes et dessins)

faces, coiffed like a rhinoceros or a royal bird."[2] Drinkers, gamblers and
duelers, they cultivated libertine behavior and eschewed emotional
entanglements with women. Attempting always to scandalize the bourgeoisie,
they made a point of rude behavior to women in general, and actresses in
particular.[3] The presence of these outrageous young men no doubt imposed
itself well beyond the force of their actual numbers, such that they alone
became identified as the type of spectator who watched a play from the stage.

Stage seats, however, were also occupied by ordinary men of station or
rank who happened to be attending the theatre alone. The social hierarchy
associated with seating in a public theatre is set forth by *Séjour de Paris,* a 1727
guidebook intended for well-off visitors to Paris. It advises that "at the theatre,
a man of quality views the play from the stage, from a lower box or from the
parterre, rarely from the second boxes, intended for the bourgeoisie, never
from the amphitheatre where all the rabble assembles."[4] Stage seats thus were
one of three socially acceptable alternatives for an unaccompanied spectator of
rank, and probably the easiest and most agreeable one. A single seat in a box
might mean intruding on a larger party, while a ticket to the *parterre* meant
standing and being jostled. A seat on the stage was a likely choice.

While the general comportment of a dominant portion of stage spectators
was outrageous even by then-prevailing standards, it is necessary, in evaluating
the impact of that comportment, to be aware of the context in which it
occurred. For a variety of reasons, the theatre-going public in the seventeenth
and eighteenth centuries behaved very differently from what we are
accustomed to today.[5] Partly the difference had to do with theatre architecture
of the time, which was not particularly conducive to concentration on the play
being performed. The indoor tennis courts *(jeux de paume)* which had housed
early theatres were rectangular in shape, with seating lined up along the lengths
of the rectangle. While optimal for watching tennis games, such an
arrangement was less so for viewing plays: spectators in the boxes faced not the
stage, but a row of boxes on the opposite side of the house. Moreover, house
lights remained illuminated throughout the performance. (Lighting, it will be
remembered, consisted of chandeliers holding numerous candles which could
not, of course, be dimmed, or turned on and off.) It was thus easier for seated
spectators to look at each other than at the actors and actresses. Spectators
standing in the *parterre* could orient themselves towards the action on stage if
they wished, but by the same token were free to move about the floor at will.

Far less inhibited and polite than today's theatre-goer, audiences talked
aloud during performances and called out comments and taunts to the actors
and to each other. A running dialogue was frequently carried on between
spectators on the stage and spectators in the *parterre.* Much of the time, the
play that was being performed was overshadowed by the by-play which
surrounded it. Indeed, the theatre represented not so much an aesthetic
experience as a social event, like a salon, a ball, an outing or even a cabaret.

People attended the theatre to see and be seen, to make contacts, flirt, circulate. Women held court in the boxes; the lorgnette was an essential piece of equipment. All of this activity was utterly independent of what was taking place on the stage: spectators frequently remained oblivious to the action behind the row of smoky candles which constituted the *rampe* or footlights.

An abundance of contemporary anecdotes and satires suggests what a visit to the theatre meant. One such is a celebrated passage in Montesquieu's *Lettres persanes.*

> Yesterday I saw a rather singular thing, even though it happens every day in Paris.
> Everybody assembles towards the end of the afternoon and goes to act out a kind of scene that I have heard referred to as a *play*. The important action takes place on a platform called the *stage*. At either side, one sees, in little nooks which are called loges, men and women playing mute scenes together, a bit like those which are customary in our Persia.
> Here, an afflicted mistress languishes; another, more animated, devours her lover with her eyes, and is devoured in turn by him: all sorts of passions are painted on their faces and expressed with an eloquence no less lively for being mute. There, the actresses can only be seen from the waist up .... Below stands a horde of people making fun of those up above on the stage: the latter in turn laugh at those below.[6]

Whatever the social opportunities enjoyed by spectators occupying the lower boxes, an even more exquisite opportunity was available to the *petits marquis* who purchased tickets to the stage. The primary aim of these ornamental young men was to be noticed, and a seat on the stage was ideal for that purpose. One of the major advantages was lighting. The presence of spectators on either side of the stage made it imperative to keep the chandeliers which hung over those areas lighted at all times. Spectators seated in those locations thus remained illuminated throughout the performance and in a position of maximum visibility. The public in the auditorium could focus as readily on the *petits-maîtres* as on the players.

Another advantage of acquiring a ticket to the stage was obligatory passage through the *foyers.* As previously noted, ingress and egress to stage seats at the Ancienne Comédie was via the *foyers* or greenrooms immediately off the queen's side of the stage (see fig. 10). The two *foyers* in question were, in the words of Blondel, "rooms meant to assemble actors and persons being seated on the stage, who, in winter, conveniently gather there before the show, and during intermissions."[7] It was here during intermissions that actors and actresses received visitors of note and special friends. The *foyers* were not public, but habitués and certain other special individuals were admitted. Gentlemen of the King's Bed Chamber, nobles who had liaisons with the actresses, and men of letters came to the *foyers* to chat with the artists during intermissions.[8] While most *petits-maîtres* no doubt fell into none of those categories, they were able to mingle, or appear to mingle, with persons of distinction in the normal course of passing to or from their seats.

A further advantage enjoyed by habitués of the stage benches was the possibility of an occasional brush with royalty, whenever princes of the blood chose to sit on the stage rather than in their boxes. Stage seats also afforded proximity to the actresses, hence the opportunity to engage in close-range flirtation in the very midst of the play. All of these factors contributed to the allure of sitting on the stage and help explain why the *petits marquis* went to the lengths they often did to gain admission to the stage.

Conscious of being in the limelight, or more accurately, the candle light, as they were, these young men tended to exaggerate the outrageous behavior for which they were noted. Virtually no attention-getting technique was overlooked: *petits-maîtres* lounged rather than sat on the stage benches; they got up and walked about during the performance, crossed the stage, entered and exited as they pleased, and did not hesitate to carry on loud conversations with each other, with the actresses, and with the *parterre*. Illustrations depicting these young men on the stage invariably show them in animated poses, with hands moving and heads turned in conversation (see particularly figs. 2, 3, 4 and 14).

Numerous contemporary texts evoke the carryings-on of the *petits-maîtres*, none perhaps more piquantly than a passage from La Morlière's 1746 novel, *Angola.*

> On the stage could be seen . . . a number of men, among them, only barely perceptible, a very few true appreciators of the merits of a play; these few sensible people did not make a public spectacle of themselves at all, and waited quietly in their seats to enjoy the tragedy; but what are called "fashionable folk" thought quite otherwise: they hardly bothered about the play, and often in Act V inquired what had been performed; immodestly reclining rather than sitting on the stage, they displayed their seductive charms, continually put up their lorgnettes, smoothed their jabots, fiddled with a bouquet, whistled a new tune, made meaningful signs to actresses who often didn't know them, and finally, having exhausted all the commonplaces of a coquetterie that would have embarrassed the most forward of women, chose the most interesting moment to walk across the stage, looking at their watches and disturbing the actors. Seemingly distracted and rushed, they exited, hurried to their carriages, and put in an appearance at all the other theatres, where they proceeded to commit the same frivolities and indecencies.[9]

If a stage-regular felt that his foppish persona alone was inadequate, he might come equipped with a prop, such as the dog brought by a marquis to a performance of Dancourt's *Trois Cousines* on November 22, 1700. A police report describes the event.

> Day before yesterday, there was an incident at the Comédie occasioned by the Danish dog that Monsieur the Marquis de Livry the younger had brought there. The dog began to do his tricks on the stage . . . [and] in order to encourage him, the gentlemen in the pit made all the hunting calls they could think of.[10]

Sometimes a *petit-maître*, having overindulged at dinner, came to the theatre bolstered by alcohol. A character in Regnard's play, *Le Distrait* (1697), directs criticism to one such:

> You pride yourself on being a frank libertine;
> Your glory rides on how well you hold your wine;
> And when, all steamy with a winey breath,
> Your shaky feet can hardly hold you up.
> It's then that you come show yourself on a stage:
> There, amongst your likes, you play the fool;
> Go around kissing each other like girls,
> And, in order to be seen on high,
> Push and bump one another, recounting your exploits,
> Raising your voice louder than the actors....[11]

If all of this behavior seems zoo-like from today's perspective, it struck at least one contemporary observer the same way. D'Allainval, in *L'Ecole des Bourgeois* (1728), constructed a fable in which a monkey invites inhabitants of the forest to the theatre to watch him perform his juggling act. Canaries and parakeets sit in the boxes, foxes are assigned to the *parterre*, while

> On the stage could be seen
> Sprawling and ogling,
> Sir Lion, Mylord Rhinoceros
> Seigneur Elephant and other such important folk.[12]

Sometimes posing and preening were not enough, and the *petits marquis* allowed excessively high spirits to get the better of them. At the first performance of Brueys and Palaprat's *Le Grondeur* in 1691 at the Comédie Française, the stage spectators seem to have comported themselves somewhat more destructively than usual.

> It pleased some of them to come to the first performance of the *Grondeur*, but not to retain self-control. There was no sort of apish antic they didn't direct at the play, not out of malice, probably, but only out of natural gaiety. All eyes were turned upon them...and no one payed further attention to the...show....The play was ultimately so discredited in the minds of high society that several days later when the late Prince wished to go to the theatre, he asked that the *Grondeur* not be given, since he had heard so much bad said of it.[13]

Though disturbance was synonymous with spectators on the stage, in at least one instance the crowd on the stage served to conceal a disruption rather than cause one. The incident, recounted by Mouhy, took place during a 1694 performance of Dancourt's *Opéra de Village*.

The Marquis de Sablé, having departed intoxicated from a long dinner, and upon hearing, in the twelfth scene of this new piece, the singing of a couplet about how vineyards and prairies will be *sablés* [sanded], was convinced that the author [Dancourt] had him in mind and that in naming him, insulted him. Seeking out the author, and finding him near a wing, the Marquis ran at him and slapped his face. Dancourt was inclined to feel insulted and draw his sword, but was prevented; friends surrounded the Marquis and led him to the greenroom. Fortunately the stage was so crowded that the *parterre* remained ignorant of the adventure....[14]

Besides its special attributes as a social event, sitting on the stage offered petty nobility the opportunity to remind itself of its own superiority. As the eighteenth century progressed, the growing prosperity of the bourgeoisie resulted in the burgeoning purchase of titles. As a result, more and more newly-arrived *petits marquis* needed every means possible to convince themselves and others that they were indeed what their titles said they were.[15] Frequently a stage ticket *(billet de théâtre)* was, so to speak, just the ticket for affirmation of social rank. Actors and actresses, while sought after socially for their reputed wit and charm, were considered of inferior rank. Excommunicated by the church and divested of civil status, theatre people, despite the glamour and wealth that sometimes surrounded them, were still viewed as little more than servants of the aristocracy.[16] Thus, those desirous of bolstering their image by referring to this relationship found it easy to do so within the context of stage seating.

An incident involving the famous actress Mademoiselle Dumesnil illustrates how such a maneuver might be carried out. On the occasion in question, the actress, playing the role of Cleopatra in *Rodogune*, had reached a dramatic high point.

On the point of expiring with convulsions of rage, Cleopatra was pronouncing the terrifying verse: 'I would curse the gods, if they rendered me unto life,' when Mlle Dumesnil felt a great fist-blow in the back from an old military man sitting on the stage. He accompanied this stroke of delirium, which interrupted the show and the actress, with these energetic words: 'Go to the devil, bitch!' When the tragedy was finished, Mlle Dumesnil thanked him for his fist-blow as if it had been the most flattering praise she had ever received.[17]

Apart from matters of social status, stage seats were convenient for confirmation of what passed in the eyes of some as intellectual status. It was virtually *de rigueur* for persons seated on the stage to pass judgment on the spectacle at hand in as contentious and ostentatious a manner as possible, as often as not a judgment exactly opposite from that of the *parterre*. Numerous anecdotes from Molière's time forward attest to the exercise of this ritual. One incident, datable to 1662, is described by the *Anecdotes dramatiques*. It suggests the haughty, contemptuous manner frequently adopted by stage spectators turned critic.

The School for Wives received mixed reactions at its premiere. Plapisson, who passed for a great intellectual, was on the stage during the performance; and at every outburst of laughter from the *parterre,* shrugged his shoulders and looked at the *parterre* with pity; and sometimes also looking at it with contempt, said aloud: Go ahead and laugh, *parterre,* go ahead and laugh.[18]

The same pattern of disruptive opposition between stage and pit is described in connection with a 1682 revival of De Visé's *Gentilhomme Guespin,* a play first performed in 1670. According to one account, "the *parterre,* having booed the play as it had at the first performance, and those on the stage, remembering that they had applauded it then, got together and treated it exactly the same way again." As a result of the ensuing uproar, "the actors did not finish the play, and have not dared to do it since."[19] Similar behavior took place at the premiere of *Le Grondeur,* which was "hissed by the stage and protected by the *parterre.*"

Brillon's *Le Théophraste moderne* (1699) evoked more such behavior on the part of the *petits-maîtres:* "First on the stage, they established a Tribunal where plays were judged fair or bad without appeal; none were found good; excellent authors lived during their time, unable to obtain their approval."[20] And, in La Morlière's *Angola,* Almaïr guides the young prince Angola in his first visit to the Opéra.

'For shame, are you jesting?' said Almaïr, 'one has one's reputation to keep up, and nothing is as dreary as listening to a play like the corner storekeeper or like a provincial fresh from the country; we people with a certain style, we are supposed to know everything; we come here to see the women, to be seen by them, we hear at most two or three scraps sanctioned by fashion, and at the end, we excessively praise or boldly condemn the entire play.'[21]

Those who populated the stage felt obliged to pass judgment on a play, though it was not good tone to pay close attention to the play, nor was it desirable to be of the same opinion as the *parterre.* If intellectual status was attainable through systematic ruination of the offerings of professional theatre, then the *petits marquis* were lofty indeed. While the antic ritual of instant praise or blame may have enhanced the status of the *petits marquis* in their own eyes, if in no one else's, it exercised undue influence on the success or failure of a play, and surely could not have been a great help to forward movement in the theatre.

Other Stage Spectators

Though the stage was normally the territory of the elite, less exalted personages sometimes could be found there. An entry in the *Anecdotes dramatiques* recounts what transpired at a 1729 performance at the Comédie Italienne when a member of the clergy ventured onto the stage.

Seeing an abbot sitting on the stage in the front rows, the *parterre* began to shout: 'Down, Mr. Abbot, down.' Calmly, the abbot remained where he was, as if this matter had nothing to do with him; but as they continued to hoot at him, he rose, and addressing the *parterre:* 'Gentlemen,' said he, 'since being robbed of a gold watch in your company, I would rather be out the price of a seat on the stage than risk being out my snuff-box.' The hooting changed to applause, and the abbot took his seat.[22]

Another anecdote, harking back to an earlier era, describes the incursion of a different element:

The story is told of an important noble wishing to play a nasty trick on Molière's troupe. Recruiting all the hunch-backs he could find on the Pont-Neuf, he gave each one a stage ticket for that evening. When the curtain rose, the public burst out laughing upon seeing left and right, under the classical porticos, two double rows of hunch-backs, one more deformed than the other.[23]

Other extraneous elements of the public could also be found on the stage from time to time. It was decided in 1697, for instance, to add to the rules for admission and seating at the Comédie Française that under certain circumstances "the children of actors will be admitted to the benches on stage."[24] And, at the Comédie Italienne pages, perhaps nostalgic for earlier custom, continued to find ways now and then to gain admission to the stage. "The king's pages and the princes' pages, having been limited to a private box in the second tier, ganged together and on various occasions forced their way past guards and supernumeraries in order to get onto the stage." On one occasion, in 1726, "they had asked for a lower box which they were refused, and since in order to get to the one they were assigned they had to go by way of the stage, they insisted on staying there." Protest was in vain: "Letters were written to their superiors, who excused them on various pretexts."[25]

On the other end of the scale, members of the court and the royal family often attended performances in the ordinary public theatres. Louis XIV's brother, Monsieur, was a frequent spectator there, as were the dauphin and his wife. Between 1680 and 1722 the Comédie Française was attended repeatedly by the Duc d'Orléans and his daughter, the Duchesse de Berry; the Duchesse du Maine; the Prince and Princesse de Conti; the Duchesse de Bourgogne; the Duc de Mantoue; the Duchesse de Bouillon; the Comte de Ponchartrain.[26] The presence of such personages attracted spectators who wished to see nobles of the court at close range. Much of the time high-ranking nobility chose to sit on the stage, rather than in the royal boxes.[27] Needless to say, the arrival on stage of a royal party had a noticeable effect on the dramatic action in progress. "Princes of the blood most often go sit on the stage," writes a contemporary, and when that happens, "the actors suspend the scene, all the spectators rise out of respect, and the princes occupy the first seats relinquished by those sitting there."[28]

In at least one exceptional instance, women sat on the stage. The occasion was Boyer's enormously successful religious play, *Judith*, performed in 1695. According to the Abbé de Villiers, such immodest behavior on the part of female spectators was due to the crowds who, clamoring to see this play, had preempted the *loges* in which women normally sat.

> It is thus that *Judith*, a shapeless tragedy,
> Shone for three months, applauded at the theatre,
> And was even, so I was told, despite its coldness,
> The first at which women were seen, immodestly
> Placed at the same level as the actors, on the stage;
> Chased from the boxes by the crowd, they went
> To occupy the stage and be laughed at,
> Preferring the hideous spectacle to missing out.[29]

The event is also described by Lesage:

> The men were obliged to relinquish the stage to them and remain standing in the wings. Imagine two hundred ladies seated on benches where ordinarily only men are to be seen, with handkerchiefs spread on their laps in order to wipe their eyes during touching moments![30]

The records confirm that during its initial performances in March 1695, *Judith* was very well attended by those who liked to sit in the best seats. On several occasions, over two hundred of the most expensive tickets were sold.[31] Women also sat on the stage during the occasional free performances offered by the Comédie Française. The seating arrangement at one of those performances, proferred as a "get well" wish for Louis XV in 1721, is described in *Le Mercure:* "At the outset it was established that women, children and old or infirm men would be admitted to the boxes, the stage and the amphitheatre, while young men and commoners would be sent to the *parterre*."[32] Women viewing a performance from the stage can also be seen on an illustration of a 1745 presentation of Voltaire and Rameau's comédie-ballet, the *Princesse de Navarre*, at Versailles (see fig. 26). The small seating area meant for stage spectators appears to be occupied by men, but women are shown standing about, as though they might have pressed forward from the wing openings.[33]

Though only exceptionally to be found on the stage proper, women were, in fact, normally present behind the curtain. The installation of stage box seating at the Guénégaud around 1676 brought about a change not only in the size of population behind the curtain but in its composition. The relative privacy afforded by the *balcons* permitted introduction of a feminine element to this territory which had until then been exclusively masculine (see fig. 14). Initially, the *balcons* were probably meant not so much for the general public as for intimates of the actors and actresses. The first and second tiers of these boxes were usually occupied by ladies and gentlemen of the aristocracy who were friends of various troupe members.[34] Later on, at the new theatre on rue des Fossés-Saint-Germain-des-Prés (the Ancienne Comédie), the third tier of stage boxes was given over to free seating for servants of the actors and actresses, each thespian household being accorded one key to those boxes.[35]

In the face of the oddity, self-promotion and general circus atmosphere that seems to have been the norm amongst occupants of the stage seats, it is almost a surprise to find that some individuals who came to the stage were motivated by the desire, pure and simple, to see the spectacle from close up. This was doubtless the case in 1685 and 1686 at the Comédie Française when, as the *registres* show, at a number of performances by the great Baron, the lower boxes were deserted and the stage overflowed. Indeed, it would be erroneous to suggest that spectators on the stage interfered with all plays at all times, or that no play was ever heard because of the carryings-on of the *petits marquis*. Surely then, as now, attentiveness to a spectacle was a function of the interest it held for the audience, and plays, as well as the actors and actresses who performed them, stood or fell on the merits perceived by public and critics. However, silence in the theatre in the seventeenth century and most of the eighteenth century was earned, not granted. Many a play was not capable of holding the young dandies in check, but some plays were. One such, according to La Morlière's *Angola*, was Voltaire's *Mérope*.

All that brilliant youth was showing off on the stage when the warning came that the show was about to begin, and, what is not an insignificant proof of the superior reputation of the play, the simpering, the disorder and the chattering ceased, and the young men prepared to listen attentively to that admirable masterpiece.[36]

It obviously required a clever playwright and experienced actors to persuade the audience, and particularly the *petits-maîtres*, to sit still and listen to the play being performed.

Aesthetic Considerations

In seeking to explain some of the behavior and motivation behind the persistent presence of spectators on the stage, one must take into account not only the status factors at play, but some aesthetic factors as well. French classical theatre, for all its theoretical purity and nobility, balance and verisimilitude, was, in terms of performance reality, still imprisoned within what might be termed a kind of living baroque framework. Although as the seventeenth century progressed, audiences might have been, indeed were, ready for the type of theatre they were getting from Corneille and Racine, they at the same time were deprived of some of the spectacular and the diverting aspects of theatre as it had been before. To be sure, the French public's continuing taste for baroque theatre was being catered to by the machine plays given at the

Marais Theatre and sometimes at the Comédie Française. But this need for spectacle more animated than that provided by classical declamation alone was no doubt also reflected in the long-term existence of spectators on the stage, and in all of the agitation, the unseemliness and lack of verisimilitude that went along with them.

The presence of spectators on the stage cannot, of course, in any sense be considered a direct manifestation of baroque theatre. But the tolerance for, and indeed encouragement of, spectators on the stage can readily be viewed as an expression of the public's desire that theatre retain some of the characteristics that have subsequently been termed baroque. Difficult as it is to define the baroque in entirely satisfactory fashion, one can nonetheless focus on certain of its significant characteristics, such as the emphasis on theatricality in the baroque era, the notion of dualism, and, in theatre itself, the penchant for visual excitement, surprise and incongruity. The continuing presence of *petits marquis* on the stage was not at all unrelated to the influence of those factors.

Theatricality as a way of leading life, and confusion of life and theatre, were dominant characteristics of the baroque age.[37] Simple acts of life were turned into theatrical ceremony: Louis XIV rising in the morning, retiring at night, taking nourishment, were theatrical events at Versailles, public performances attended by the privileged. Public display of luxurious possessions, particularly clothing, was a preoccupation at all levels of society.[38] The *petits marquis* who populated the stage were engaged in exactly this kind of theatricality and display. Parading their finery, turning flirtation into a public ceremony, they were engaging in a theatrical act, carried out on the stage of the Comédie Française, no less. For the *petits marquis* who night after night made the rounds of Paris stages, who lived illuminated by stage lights, life remained theatre and theatre remained life well beyond the waning of the baroque era.

Another contributing factor might be described as lingering nostalgia for baroque-style complexity or duality. Frequently in the baroque universe there is juxtaposition of two effects which do not seem to belong together, which appear divergent and disorderly, but which in reality obey strict rules of thought and ultimately converge towards a unified end.[39] The continuing intrusion of spectators on the stage in tandem with Corneille, Racine and Molière was nothing if not such a dualistic phenomenon. The disorderly behavior of spectators on the stage surely could not have seemed more in opposition or more at cross-purposes to official performances of classical theatre pieces. Yet such apparent incoherence was in a deeper sense quite coherent and logical, for the focus of both the spectators on the stage and the actors on the stage was the spectacle at hand and the pleasure of the public. And certainly the public continued to perceive its pleasure in precisely those baroque terms, else the presence of the *petits marquis* on the premier stage of France could not have been tolerated as long as it was.

What the public had probably enjoyed most in baroque theatre was its visual excitement. Fashioned for the eye as much as for the ear, baroque theatre had offered movement, color, spectacle—elements purged from classical theatre. It is striking that as French theatre grew more and more static *visually* (though certainly not emotionally or psychologically), the presence of spectators on the stage grew more and more animated, surely in some sense compensating the public for the baroque spectacle that had been shunted aside: And if yet another characteristic of baroque theatre was misunderstanding, surprise effect and incongruity, it is hard to imagine what could be more surprising or incongruous than a cavorting dog or a thump on the back in the midst of a serious play.

Despite the occasional incursions of other spectators—the sincere, the women, the children, the pages, the abbots and the deformed, the stage remained overwhelmingly the territory of petty nobility. Territorial prerogative was established and maintained not by regulation, or even so much by pricing, as by social barriers, since those who gravitated towards the stage were drawn there for compelling social reasons. It is moreover ironic, and perhaps more than incidentally significant, that the earliest recorded instance of the seating of spectators on the stage occurs with the earliest performances of the very play credited with bridging the gap between baroque theatre and classical theatre. Had it not been for the simultaneous decor still being used in early performances of the *Cid*—a decor affording convenient *niches* between *mansions*—those first courtiers might have found it much less convenient to install themselves on the stage. Yet, spectators on the stage as a formalized custom did not exist so long as baroque theatre held sway. Only as the cluttered plays of Théophile, Jean de Schelandre and others disappeared from view did this extracurricular spectacle along the sides of the stage move in to fill the void. The pure verse and noble sentiment of Corneille's heros and Racine's heroines were thus always offset by the most impure and ignoble of backdrops—the activity of dozens, and eventually hundreds, of posing, preening *petits marquis*.

4

The Magnitude of Stage Seating and Its Economics

Important as social and aesthetic factors were in keeping so many *petits marquis* on the stage for so long in the seventeenth and eighteenth centuries, what really counted, then as now, was the so-called bottom line. If theatre troupes did not always act as forcefully as they might have to control the number of spectators on the stage, it was surely because having them there had proven so lucrative. And because stage spectators generated a disproportionate amount of revenue for the Paris theatre troupes, the early limits adhered to during Molière's time gradually yielded to the pressure for more stage seating. *Balcons* or stage boxes were soon introduced as a supplement to seats on the stage proper, while the institution of *entrées gratuites* or free admissions further swelled the number of spectators behind the curtain. At the Ancienne Comédie, permanent stage seating for paying customers was greatly expanded over the years until its ultimate ridiculous magnitude was reached.

Early Limits

In the early decades, the practice of seating spectators on the stage was not as intrusive as it was later to become. If the troupe's last season at the Palais Royal as recorded in the *Registre d'Hubert* is indicative, Molière's theatre limited the number of stage spectators to thirty-two, or at least did not regularly sell more than that number of stage tickets. The only exception was the first performance of a play by a friend of the troupe (Donneau de Visé), *Les Maris infidèles*, when thirty-six stage tickets were sold—an honor which did not forestall the play's immmediate failure.[1] Otherwise, the number of stage tickets sold by Molière's troupe during the year covered by the *Registre* never exceeded thirty-two, even after his death.[2] If Molière's troupe, deprived of its leader, and doubtless worried about the future, continued nonetheless to limit sales of these lucrative tickets to thirty-two, it is likely that this was a well-established maximum.

Table I. Stage Ticket Sales and Receipts, 1672-1686

Theatre	Season	Number of Performances[a]	Maximum Number of Stage Tickets per Performance[b]	Average Number of Stage Tickets per Performance[c]	Average Receipts per Performance (*livres*)[d]
Troupe du Roi Molière Palais-Royal	1672-73	131	36	10	685
	1673-74	108	40	10	471
	1674-75	145	40	9	609
	1675-76	146	44	11	701
Troupe du Roi Hôtel Guénégaud	1676-77	131	80	11	464
	1678-79	165	87	18	374
	1679-80	182	135	48	669

1680-81	642	55	150	287	
1681-82	601	45	124	320	
1682-83	632	42	120	351	
Comédie Française					
1683-84	501	28	103	282	
Hôtel Guénégaud					
1684-85	522	36	112	352	
1685-86	552	36	203	328	

[a] *Number of Performances.* The 287 performances indicated for 1680-81 include the 77 given by the Troupe du Roi before its merger with the Hôtel de Bourgogne. The Comédie Française performed 210 times during that first season.

[b] *Maximum Number of Stage Tickets per Performance.* The play and the date for each maximum are: *Les Maris infidèles*, January 24, 1673 (36); *Le Comédien poète*, November 10, 1673 and *La Mort d'Achille*, December 31, 1673 (40); *Dom César d'Avalos*, December 21, 1674 (40); *Iphigénie*, June 7, 1675 (44); *Phèdre et Hippolyte*, January 22, 1677 (80); *Monsieur de Pourceaugnac* and *Georges Dandin*, February 22, 1678 (70); *Tartuffe*, January 8, 1679 (87); *La Devineresse*, February 4, 1680 (135); *Phèdre*, opening night of the Comédie Française, August 25, 1680, *La Mère coquette*, January 19, 1681, *Le Misanthrope*, February 17, 1681 and *Horace*, March 2, 1681 (150); *Le Misanthrope*, January 31, 1682 (124); *Le Malade imaginaire*, March 1, 1683 (120); *Le Malade imaginaire*, February 14, 1684 (103); *La Fille capitaine*, February 11, 1685, *Andronic*, February 12 and March 19, 1685 (112); *Alcibiade*, February 10, 1686 (203).

[c] *Average Number of Stage Tickets per Performance.* Averages were obtained by dividing the total number of *billets de théâtre* sold each season by the number of performances. Daily figures appearing in the *registres* were added to arrive at totals. Two seasons, 1674-75 and 1675-76, were considered as a special case because of the incidence of machine plays for which performances spectators were generally not allowed on the stage. Performances for which stage tickets were not put on sale have thus been eliminated in calculating these averages. This involved nine performances of *Circé* in 1674-75 and seventy-two performances of *Circé* and the *Inconnu* in 1675-76. If these performances had been included, the average number of stage tickets sold would have been eight in 1674-75 and six in 1675-76. During subsequent seasons, the *registres* show the sale of *billets de théâtre* for machine plays, almost certainly for newly-installed stage boxes, and those figures have been included.

[d] *Average Receipts per Performance.* Average receipts were obtained by dividing total ticket sales for each season by the number of performances. Ticket sale figures for 1672-73 were taken from S. Chevalley's *Registre d'Hubert* for 1673-80 and *Registre de La Grange* and from Claude Alasseur's *La Comédie Française au IIe siècle: étude économique* (Paris: Mouton, 1967), p. 135.

The new Troupe du Roi, installed at the Hôtel Guénégaud and consisting of some of the former members of Molière's troupe and the entire Marais troupe (and probably dominated by La Grange and his friends, judging by its repertory), seems to have maintained about the same modest limit with regard to stage spectators. As can be seen in table 1 above, the *registres* for 1673-74 and 1674-75 show that the actors never sold more than forty stage tickets, a maximum attained only three times during those two seasons.[3] In 1675-76, the largest number of stage tickets sold was forty-four. Calculation of the average number of stage tickets or *billets de théâtre* sold confirms that the number of spectators admitted to the stage remained quite modest during that period. During Molière's last season, there was an average of ten spectators on the stage, and this number remained fairly constant for several years after the remains of his troupe joined with the Marais troupe: ten in 1673-74; nine in 1674-75; eleven in 1775-76; eleven in 1676-77.

The Hôtel de Bourgogne probably followed about the same policy. From a 1666 engraving representing a portion of that stage and showing some twenty-five spectators sitting and standing, the presence of about forty spectators can be extrapolated (see fig. 15). The fifteen or so spectators depicted as standing may well have been admitted to the stage without a ticket, for numerous dignitaries were entitled to free admission to Paris theatres.[4] By the same token, the other theatres surely also admitted standees in excess of the maximum thirty-two tickets sold. In any case, forty or fifty spectators occupying the stages of Molière's theatre, the Marais Theatre, the Hôtel de Bourgogne, or the Guénégaud were a far cry from the hundreds that were to populate the stage of the Comédie Française in the following century.

Balcons or Stage Boxes

The installation of box seats on the stage was an early move designed to accommodate more spectators in the choice area behind the curtain. Unlike the seating known today as *loges d'avant scène*, located in front of the curtain, these new boxes, called *balcons*, were located behind the curtain.[5] They constituted an extension onto the stage of the rows of regular boxes, and probably consisted of a bank of two boxes on each side, stacked two or three high. (see figs. 6, 8, 9, 14 and 20). The *registres* unfortunately do not yield a great deal of information about these boxes because ticket sales for both stage seats proper and *balcons* were normally lumped together under the THEATRE category. From time to time, however, handwritten entries regarding *balcon* tickets do occur in the *registres* such that certain conclusions can be drawn.

While it does not seem that the Palais Royal offered this type of seating (the *Registre d'Hubert* does not show the sale of tickets for such seats), there is evidence that the Hôtel Guénégaud did have *balcons*. The *registre* for February

Figure 15. Extrapolation, *Noce de village* Illustration

26, 1677 mentions rental of "deux balcons de 33 £" for the performance of *Don Juan* on that date.[6] Five years later, the account book for 1682-83 regularly indicates the sale of tickets for the "théâtre et balcon," the "balcon and loges," or simply the "balcon." Besides this, the record for January 27, 1686 shows the sale of 190 "theatre et balcon" tickets for a performance of *Alcibiade*. There can be no doubt, then, about the existence of stage boxes at the Guénégaud.

What is less clear, however, is the date of their installation. Despite the absence of confirming documents, it seems likely that *balcons* were introduced to the Guénégaud just prior to 1676-77, the season during which they are mentioned for the first time in the *registres*. The numbers appear to bear this out: tabulation of the maximum number of stage seats sold during a given season (table 1) shows that prior to 1676-77 the number of paid admissions to the stage never exceeded forty-four, whereas during that season the maximum reached eighty and never thereafter fell below seventy.

It is not difficult to imagine why the actors and actresses might have desired to install boxes behind the curtain. For one, the exclusion of spectators from the stage during performances of machine plays must have displeased some of the best customers. Not only had the *petits marquis* grown accustomed to being part of the spectacle themselves, they doubtless also wished to observe the mysteries of the machines from up close. For another, the actors surely regretted the loss of revenue from these lucrative seats. By installing boxes on the stage, the troupe could, without interfering with the machines, both please these spectators and maintain revenues.

Records for the 1682-83 season at the Guénégaud are particularly informative about the stage boxes. Entries pertaining to the revival of *Andromède*, an old success of Pierre Corneille's, clearly confirm that during performances of machine plays, spectators who purchased stage tickets sat in the *balcons* but not on the *banquettes*. The records for *Andromède*, a play which relied on a whole range of mechanical effects and required total exclusion of spectators from the stage, are revealing because of the special way they were kept. Obviously more precise than most of his colleagues, the troupe member in charge of the *registres* at that moment carefully modified the printed form. Since no one was to be seated on the stage proper during *Andromède*, on each page for that play he crossed out the printed word THEATRE (stage), and wrote in by hand the word "Balcon." We thus know that spectators who bought *billets de théâtre* for *Andromède* were placed exclusively in stage boxes.

The 1682-83 records are even more helpful insofar as they indicate that under normal circumstances both *balcon* tickets and *banquette* tickets (stage box and stage bench tickets) were entered under the same category. Except for *Andromède*, there were spectators on the stage at all plays given that season, and so our record-keeper, always precise, added the word "Balcon" to the printed form, thereby creating a "Theatre et balcon" (stage and stage box) category.

At the Hôtel Guénégaud, there were probably close to one hundred seats in the boxes behind the curtain, judging from "balcon" entries that go as high as eighty and one hundred for certain performances.[7] There is no real information about the configuration of these stage boxes, but it is not unreasonable to suppose that it resembled what the Comédie Française would use several years later (1689) in their new theatre on the rue des Fossés-Saint-Germain-des-Prés. That theatre had twelve stage boxes altogether: six on each side of the stage, arrayed in three tiers of two boxes each (see fig. 6). As for the capacity of the stage boxes at the Guénégaud, we know that certain of them were intended to hold only six persons, as opposed to the eight spectators in regular boxes. In the *registre* for February 26, 1677, an entry under *loges* indicates that in addition to the rental of four regular boxes at 44 £ each, there were also "deux balcons de 33 £," for a total of 242 £. Since the most expensive seats at that time sold for 5 £ 10s, it can be readily calculated that the stage boxes in question held six persons.[8] However, to arrive plausibly at a total of eighty or one hundred places in these boxes, it is necessary to postulate that some of them held more than six spectators. Analogous to what would later exist at the Ancienne Comédie, where half the stage boxes held eight persons and the other half held ten,[9] one can suppose that only half the stage boxes at the Guénégaud held six, while the other half held eight or even ten spectators. Such configurations would have resulted in a total of eighty-four or ninety-six stage box seats. Since the capacity of any box was somewhat elastic,[10] the two hypotheses seem equally plausible. Adding these upper and lower limits for stage box seats (84 and 96) to the upper and lower limits for stage seats proper (40 and 44), one arrives at a total of from 124 to 140 seats behind the curtain of the Hôtel Guénégaud.

It is, of course, not possible to ascertain exactly how many of the spectators who purchased stage tickets at the Guénégaud were sitting in the stage boxes and how many on the stage benches. There is no way of knowing, for example, how many of the 120 "théâtre et balcon" tickets sold for the May 1, 1683 performance of the *Malade imaginaire* were bought by noisy, ostentatious *petits marquis* desirous of disporting themselves on the *banquettes,* and how many by persons wishing to sit within the shelter of the *balcons.* If the foregoing hypothetical figures are admitted, however, the forty to forty-four places on the stage itself only represent about one-third of the total number of stage tickets that could be sold. Though almost nothing is known about the physical layout of the Guénégaud, there is an indication that the width of the stage at the front was standard for the time. This indication is based on a scale representing *toises* marked off on Joachim Pizzoli's sketch for the décor of *Psyché,* revived at the Guénégaud in October of 1684. According to the drawing, the stage of the Guénégaud had a ten-meter opening at the front.[11] In terms of stage space, this would have put the Guénégaud in about the same position as the Hôtel de Bourgogne, and later, the Ancienne Comédie.

While it is true that starting in 1676 larger numbers of stage tickets than before were regularly sold (table 1), this resulted, as has been shown, from the installation of stage boxes behind the curtains, rather than from an increase in the number of seats on the stage itself. Remembering that about two-thirds of the spectators who bought stage tickets were probably seated not on the benches but in the boxes, it can be seen that the Troupe du Roi continued to practice essentially the same restraint as had Molière with regard to stage seating. Even after formation of the Comédie Française in 1680 (by a merger of the Troupe du Roi and the Hôtel de Bourgogne players), these limits seem for the most part to have been observed.

One notable exception was the 1685-86 season, when certain performances by the popular actor Michel Baron elicited the sale of extraordinary numbers of stage tickets. In December of 1685 and January and February of 1686, sales of this category of tickets sometimes reached 172, 174, 175, 183, 190 and, on one occasion, 203. These phenomenal sales were generated by two plays: Campistron's *Alcibiade,* a very successful tragedy, and *L'Homme à bonne fortune,* the first comedy of character since Molière. Though both plays were enhanced by the great Baron's acting, the second was of particular interest, since Baron was not only its star, but its author.[12] Curiously, the records show that at all of these performances, the lower boxes were nearly deserted. One must conclude that the patrons who normally occupied those seats had abandoned them in favor of crowding behind the curtain to observe the great Baron as closely as possible. Since the stage boxes could accommodate no more than eighty-four or ninety-six of these ticket-holders, the remaining eighty to one hundred or more must have been on the stage proper, many no doubt seated on extra chairs or temporary benches and many others standing.[13]

It would appear that, increased sales of stage tickets and the great Baron notwithstanding, stage seating at the Guénégaud—apart, of course, from the addition of boxes—remained essentially what it had been at the Palais Royal: two rows of benches on either side of the stage accommodating about forty spectators, supplemented on occasion by temporary seats. At the same time, seating within the stage area had been augmented. The stage boxes, though not without their minor problems (which will be discussed in the next chapter), were here to stay. They created handsome revenue, while at the same time accommodating influential people. The *balcons* marked but the beginning of a trend that would call for creation of more and more private and special seating in Parisian public theatres, much of it behind the curtain.

Free Admission

It is necessary, in attempting to evaluate the numeric record, to take into account the presence on stage of non-paying spectators—those who, for one reason or another, were entitled to free admission *(entrée gratuite)* to the various theatres. The *registres*, for all their seeming precision, only inform us about the *sale* of stage tickets, hence reflect only the number of spectators who paid to sit on the stage. In reality, a considerable number of free passes were available to the public, despite numerous rules and royal ordinances forbidding people to enter theatres without paying. A whole assortment of personages—musketeers, Gentlemen of the King's Bed Chamber, commissioners, secretaries—enjoyed the privilege of free entry throughout the seventeenth and eighteenth centuries. It is estimated that the number of people officially privileged to dispense with payment varied, over the years, from one hundred to five hundred at any given time.[14] To these offically recognized entitlements must be added relatives and guests of the actors and actresses, as well as authors and their guests. Lagrave calculates for the first part of the eighteenth century that in addition to the daily average paid attendance of 402 at the Comédie Française, there were an additional 67 non-paying spectators.[15] In other words, about seventeen percent of the audience were not paying customers. Did these non-paying spectators sit on the stage? A 1688 bylaw of the Comédie Française, detailing abuses committed, complains that "the usherettes indiscriminately place... on the stage, in the boxes and in the amphitheatre... all sorts of individuals who pay nothing at all, even domestics...."[16] Since spectators privileged to enter free of charge were, at that time, permitted to occupy any available seat,[17] it is reasonable to suppose that many of them preferred the prestigious seats on the stage, and did not, moreover, hesitate to stand on the stage when the stage benches were full.[18] This permissiveness was eventually curtailed. Less illustrious freeloaders were relegated to the amphitheatre, the section to which "actors and authors, performers from the provinces and various persons with whom [the troupe] have relations" were granted free entry.[19] However, in most instances, the number of paid admissions to the stage recorded in the account books must not be interpreted as corresponding to the number of spectators actually present on the stage, for this number was often swelled by numerous free admissions.

At the Ancienne Comédie

Evicted from the Hôtel Guénégaud, the Comédie Française moved into its new theatre on the rue des Fossés-Saint-Germain-des-Prés (today rue de l'Ancienne Comédie) in 1689. Upon opening, the theatre had two rows of *gradins* or tiered benches running along either side of the stage, backed up against the front of the stage boxes and enclosed by a balustrade. The 1690 Le Pautre engraving which served as frontispiece to Boursault's *Fables d'Esope* illustrates the general appearance of these elements (fig. 6). Judging from an unpublished account book kept by La Grange, as well as from this Le Pautre engraving, the total capacity of these benches was in the neighborhood of forty.[20]

However, there is evidence that at times significantly more than this number of spectators paid for admission to the stage. Stage tickets were no longer recorded separately on a routine basis, but on occasions when stage seat prices were increased, special entries had to be made. Thus, for instance, the *registres* indicate that on November 29, 1694 as well as on January 19, 1696, sixty-six tickets at 5 £ 10s were sold, and that sixty-nine of the specially priced tickets were sold on February 3, 1696. Since seats in the lower boxes remained at 3 £, the 5 £ 10s tickets could only have been for stage seats, and so we can assume sixty-six and sixty-nine stage seats.

When no price differential exists, estimates of the number of stage spectators can sometimes be arrived at indirectly. If for performances when very large numbers of the most expensive tickets were sold, the number of tickets for all possible lower box seats is subtracted (196 according to Lagrave's count), the number of most-expensive tickets remaining should approximate the minimum number of paid admissions to the stage.[21] At opening night of the new theatre (April 18, 1689), for example, the *registre* shows the sale of 267 individual tickets at three *livres* each, and of tickets for four eight-seat lower boxes. Thus 299 of the best seats are accounted for (32 box seats plus 267 individual seats). Subtracting the 196 possible box seats, there remains a minimum of 103 spectators on the stage for opening night. Extra benches and chairs were doubtless employed, and standees must have been numerous. This kind of extravagant number was not reached again until the March 1695 performances of *Judith* discussed in an earlier chapter, at which from 110 to 140 women were seated on the stage. A survey of the records for other performances with peak attendance between 1689 and the closing of the Comédie Italienne in May of 1697—an event which created new pressures on the Comédie Française—suggests that, save for a handful of occasions, the number of spectators on the stage did not generally exceed forty or forty-two.

After the departure of the Comédie Italienne, demand for stage seating mounted. Moreover, the void left by the absence of the Italian players was exacerbated by the fact that stage seating had recently been discontinued at the Opéra (see chapter 6). The result was that by the 1697-98 season, the Comédie Française had become the only theatre in town whose stage was still available to the *petits marquis*. The pressure for stage seating, especially during the normally heavily attended winter season, must have been perceived as intolerable, because on January 20, 1698, the troupe decided to create more of it. The minutes *(feuille d'assemblée)* for that date record a decision to "extend the balustrade" in accordance with a sketch presented by the actor Paul Poisson, who was directed to do with the "tiered benches . . . as he shall deem best."

In the absence of supporting documents, the precise moment and manner in which stage seating was increased remains unknown. The improvements might have been accomplished very quickly on February 4, 1698 when for unexplained reasons the troupe did not perform.[22] Or perhaps the modifications were not undertaken until the Easter recess. There is no real information about the nature of the added seating, but it is probable that not all of the rows of benches shown on the Blondel plan were installed at this time. In all likelihood, Poisson merely arranged for the extension of the front bench on either side of the stage, without attempting to add more benches within the balustrade, as would be done at a later time. In any case, it is quite clear from the *registres* that from this time forward, more people than ever before were purchasing the best tickets, that is, tickets for the first tier of box seats, or for the stage boxes or stage benches.

The *registres* show also that the troupe was taking a special interest in its stage seating at this time. During the winter season of 1698-99, from December 9 to March 4, the players raised the price of stage seats from the usual 3 £ to 5 £ 10s, and, perforce, recorded them separately, in this instance clearly designated as *billets de théâtre*.[23] Throughout this period there were frequently sixty or seventy or as many as eighty-five spectators who paid to sit on the stage. The fact that 85 is the highest number of stage tickets recorded, and that this was for a crowded performance (February 28, with over 1100 tickets sold, including five lower boxes and 144 tickets at 3 £ in addition to the 5 £ 10s stage seats), tends to confirm that the stage seating shown by Blondel (140 places) had not yet been devised.

The increase in seating capacity of the stage of the Comédie Française responded not only to increasing numbers of spectators, but to changing tastes. As long as the public remained interested in seeing *grand spectacle* at the Comédie Française, space at the sides of the stage had to be kept available to accommodate the necessary machinery and equipment. Limiting stage seating was therefore a necessity. But once machine plays were dropped from the repertory, there was no compelling reason to continue to restrict the number of spectators on the stage. Two of the most expensive and elaborate machine plays, *Andromède* and the *Toison d'or*, received their final performances in 1683 and 1684 respectively at the Guénégaud and were never revived at the new theatre,[24] though *Psyché* and *Circé* did enjoy a rather lengthy revival there. (The latter play received eighty-four performances between 1703 and 1708). After that, however, the Parisian public seems to have tired of such spectacles, or at least was content to leave them to the Opéra, in favor of straight dramatic fare at the Comédie Française. Blondel's *Architecture Française* discusses the augmentation of stage seating at the Comédie Française.

The French nation's love for the theatre we are describing—as much for the excellence of its dramatic works as for the superiority of its actors—together with the auditorium having become much too small for the number of spectators, is no doubt the reason that the Comédie Française got rid of its machines. That circumstance then decided them to increase the number of seats in the house by installing these benches on the stage....[25]

It is not known exactly when the full four and one-half rows of stage seating shown on the Blondel plan were finally installed on the stage of the Ancienne Comédie. The *comédiens* were reponsive to pressure to increase choice seating. During the Easter recess of 1714, seats were apparently added in or near the orchestra pit. One of D'Argenson's police reports instructs a subordinate to "find out about the new seats that the troupe has introduced above the orchestra. Explain . . . how one reaches them, etc."[26] This may or may not have been the moment at which the number of places in the orchestra pit proper was increased to forty. As for the stage itself, however, there is evidence that a large increase in seating was not made until after 1715. An upholsterer's bill dated November 11, 1715 asks payment for "having upholstered the four tiered benches [*gradins*] which are on the stage for the occasion of Mr. Poisson's return."[27] This document suggests that there were still only two rows of benches on either side of the stage—four benches altogether—in the autumn of 1715, when the actor Paul Poisson returned to the Comédie Française.[28] On the other hand, the *registres* indicate that for three closing performances *(Polyeucte* in all three cases) prior to that year, there were very large numbers of spectators on the stage. On March 20, 1706, there is an entry showing the sale of "185 half-louis tickets at 6 £ 17s 6d," a price higher than either the boxes or the amphitheatre. These could only have been stage seats. Likewise, on March 16, 1709, 136 tickets were sold at 7 £ 4s, and on March 21, 1711, 159 were sold at that price.

Perhaps the remaining rows of stage seating were installed in time for the beginning of the 1716 season, the earliest opportunity after Louis XIV's death that the theatre-loving Régence would have had to effect such changes. (It was at precisely this moment, it will be remembered, that, turning its attention to matters theatrical, the Régence had recalled the Italian players from exile.) In any case, at some point the double rows of tiered benches *(gradins)* which had for so long constituted stage seating at the Comédie Française were replaced by five rows of benches, of which four were free-standing and one backed against the stage boxes. The exact configuration of this seating can be seen in figures 9 and 10. At the cost of a somewhat radical shrinkage of the space available to actors—the stage opening was "reduced to 15 *pieds* at the front and to 11 at the opposite end"—this change created enough permanent seating for 140 spectators.[29]

As we have seen, however, 140 preening noblemen on stage was not necessarily the upper limit. A 1759 entry in Barbier's *Journal* informs us that at important performances "another row of benches was added along the front of the balustrade, and, besides that, there were another fifty persons or more standing, without seats, at the back of the stage, forming a semicircle."[30] The accuracy of Barbier's account can be verified by scrutiny of the *registres* for the most crowded performances. At the closing performance on March 16, 1720, for instance, for the usual *Polyeucte*, the register shows the sale of 271 tickets at 8 £. Since all twenty-four of the lower boxes had been rented as units, and since amphitheatre seats can be accounted for in another price range, it must be assumed that the 271 premium-price tickets were for seats on the stage and in the orchestra. Subtracting 40 for the number of places in the orchestra,[31] one is left with 231 admissions to the stage—a figure which, a bit of arithmetic reveals, is in virtually exact accord with Barbier's description.[32] If to the 230 or so spectators on the stage proper are added the capacity of the stage boxes, one arrives at a possible total of some 325 spectators behind the curtain of the Comédie Française![33]

The Economic Importance of Stage Seats

Though the presence and behavior of *petits marquis* on the stages of Paris theatres was deplored by serious critics and tellingly satirized by Molière, Montesquieu, Voltaire and a host of others, there was no denying that the practice of seating spectators on the stage was a lucrative one indeed. It did not take long for the *comédiens* to comprehend that fashionable gentlemen of the aristocracy, as well as their imitators, were willing to pay dearly for the privilege of being seen in the right place at the Comédie or the Opéra. Though theatre troupes had not initially considered space on the stage as a source of revenue (only lowly authors and pages had ever cared to view plays from such an unsatisfactory vantage point, and they had done so gratis), it would seem that the economic potential of this space was instantly recognized. But because old habits die hard, especially among freeloaders, it became necessary to enunciate rules. In 1698 the Comédie Française resolved to relegate all non-paying spectators to the amphitheatre, stating that "Authors and others who are admitted without charge ... will kindly sit in the amphitheatre in order to leave the stage free for paying customers."[34]

Prices for seats on the stage appear to have been set the same as prices for seats in the best boxes. We have already cited Tallement des Réaux, who, writing in 1657, observed that "Box seats are quite expensive, and one must think of them ahead of time; for an *écu* or for half a louis one can be on the stage...." While Tallement's statement possibly suggests that stage seats at that point were less expensive and more readily available than box seats, the more likely meaning is that boxes were sold as a unit only, such that if a single gentleman was not with a party, it was cheaper and easier to buy one seat on the stage than to undertake rental of an entire box. The price of a ticket to the pit *(parterre)* of the Hôtel de Bourgogne a year later was fifteen sous[35] and if we assume that Paris theatres tended to remain competitive with one another, this would mean that, at the price of one *écu* (6 £), or a half-louis (5 £ 12½s), stage seats were more than seven times more expensive than the cheapest entry.

It appears that the going price for stage seats at Paris theatres remained at a demi-louis for a while thereafter. When the Opéra, sometime after its beginning in 1669, began allowing spectators on its stage, the price of stage tickets there must also have been a demi-louis, since, according to Du Tralage,

Lully subsequently "doubled the price of these seats to a gold louis." According to the *Registre d'Hubert*, this same ratio was in effect in 1672-73 at Molière's theatre, where the price of a stage ticket was 5 £ 10s, while that of the least expensive ticket was fifteen sous. And Furetière's 1690 *Dictionnaire universel*, under the entry for "Théâtre," says that "the seats on the stage cost half a gold louis."

For a time after Molière's death, the same prices obtained at the Hôtel Guénégaud. However, starting in 1676 the Guénégaud troupe began to experiment with a three-*livres billet de théâtre*. This became the normal price for that category of ticket beginning with the 1678-79 season, and the Comédie Française, after its formation in 1680, retained the same pricing structure. Since a *parterre* ticket remained at fifteen sous, the ratio of the most expensive to the least expensive seat prices was reduced from over seven to one to four to one.

At the Comédie Italienne, on the other hand, if Du Tralage's reporting is accurate, stage seat prices were not reduced until some time later. In 1688 it was still necessary to pay "an *écu* for seats . . . on the stage . . . and 15 sous in the *parterre*."[36] But sometime before its exile in 1697, the Italian troupe adopted the same pricing policy as the Comédie Française, lowering the cost of a stage seat to three *livres*.[37]

Though prices, as might be expected, were adjusted over the years, at the Comédie Française the four to one ratio between the price of a stage seat and the price of an entry to the *parterre* was maintained with only the most minor of deviations for the next seventy years, until 1753. Starting in September of 1753, the ordinary price for a stage ticket was raised to six *livres*, making it six times more expensive than a *parterre* ticket, which for some time had been fixed at one *livre*.[38]

Whenever an appropriate excuse presented itself, these prices were doubled and occasionally even tripled. Performances of new plays were generally priced *au double*, which meant that prices for all seats, including those on the stage, were twice what they ordinarily were. Usage varied, however. Until 1732, the price of a stage seat at an *au double* performance varied from 5 £ 12s to 8 £, except on March 17, 1714 for the closing performance of *Polyeucte*, when those seats fetched 9 £ 10s. (This all time high price was paid for 127 stage tickets.) In 1732, a regulation imposed by the ever more interfering Gentlemen of the Chambre decreed that at performances of new plays prices could no longer be doubled, but increased by only fifty percent, a practice that came to be known as *tiercer*.[39] Sometimes a seat on the stage cost more than one in a lower box. Sometimes prices were not raised at all, or were raised only for seats on the stage.[40]

After Molière's time the price of stage seats was frequently increased on occasions when visitors of great distinction were in attendance. When the Elector of Bavaria attended in November of 1709, prices were doubled on the stage and, six days later, throughout the house.[41] The *registres* of the Comédie Française indicate visits by a large assortment of French and foreign royalty, nobility and dignitaries. In regular attendance between 1680 and 1722 were the Duc d'Orléans and his daughter, the Duchesse de Berry; the Duchesse du Maine; the Prince and Princesse de Conti; the Duchesse de Bourgogne; the Duc de Mantoue; the Duchesse de Bouillon and the Comte de Ponchartrain. Turkish envoys attended twice in June 1706.[42] On such occasions, stage seats sometimes brought even higher prices than the boxes, thanks no doubt to the allure of reflected royal glory.

Paradoxical as it may seem, prices for stage sets were sometimes increased for performances of machine plays. For the run of *Psyché* in January 1704, in what amounted to one of the last gasps of this type of spectacle, spectators wishing to observe the mechanical equipment from close up paid 7 £, nearly double the normal 3 £ 12s for stage seats.[43]

Stage seats, then, were expensive, costing ordinarily four to seven times as much as admission to the *parterre*, and on many occasions bringing in double or more their usual price.

Not surprisingly, stage seats accounted for a significant portion of ticket receipts. In terms of attendance figures, the *parterre* dominated, of course, but in terms of revenues, spectators sitting in the most expensive seats, though few in number, brought in more money. During Molière's last season, stage tickets accounted for eight percent of receipts for the year (table 1), yet represented only about three percent of the theatre's capacity.[44] When the house was full, stage seats accounted for an even higher percentage of receipts. At the November 11, 1672 revival of *Psyché*, where at 872, paid attendance was among the highest of the season, the 32 spectators on the stage accounted for under four percent of attendance, but over twelve percent of receipts. (Of the total 1,442 £ 10s taken in at that performance, 176 £ were for stage seats.)

At the Guénégaud, the average annual percentage of receipts generated by stage seats remained roughly the same as for Molière's last year (see table 1). Remembering that stage tickets *(billets de théâtre)* included stage boxes *(balcons)* at the Guénégaud (starting from 1676 at least), and that of those tickets, stage seats accounted for about one-third *(balcons* for about two-thirds), it can be seen that, particularly after 1680 (the year of the formation of the Comédie Française), spectators on the stage continued to bring in about eight percent of receipts.

At the Comédie Française, after the expansion of stage seating to four and one-half rows of benches on either side, the 140 permanent seats thus created constituted 9.3 percent of the total capacity of the house, (calculated by Lagrave at about 1,500 persons).[45] When the two extra benches mentioned by Barbier were added in front of the balustrades (twenty-eight additional places by my calculation), this percentage rose to 11.2. When, in defiance of the regulations, additional tickets were sold to standees (Barbier mentions fifty as not unusual), this figure was higher. (Like the *parterre*, and unlike the boxes, the number of stage admissions that could be sold was frequently flexible in an upward direction, an attribute surely appreciated by business-minded troupes.) So at performances where the theatre was very full, with the stage presumably occupied to capacity, the contribution from spectators on the stage was very high indeed. For instance, on February 18, 1730, at the premiere of Piron's *Calisthène*, the 1,476 paying spectators created receipts of 4,574 £ 10s. The *registres* show that 437 individual tickets in the most expensive category (six *livres*) were sold. Not all of these were for stage seats, of course, but it can be calculated that some 233 of them very likely were.[46] (This would break down to 140 spectators on the permanent benches, 28 on the extra benches and 66 standees—quite in line with Barbier's description). At 6 £ each, the 233 stage admissions would have amounted to 1,398 £, or one-third of the day's receipts. An even more certain example is afforded by the record for March 16, 1720 (*Polyeucte* at closing), a date for which all twenty-four lower boxes were rented as units. The entry shows the sale of 271 tickets in the most expensive category, doubled to eight *livres* on that occasion. Assuming that 40 of these tickets were for seats in the orchestra section, and subtracting accordingly, the number of spectators on the stage would have amounted to 231. Thus while stage spectators represented no more than approximately sixteen percent of the 1,466 paid admissions, they accounted for nearly twenty-nine percent of total receipts (1,848 £ out of 6,395 £ total).

When one considers revenues from the *balcons* or stage boxes as well, the economic importance of spectators behind the curtain becomes even more impressive. All told, behind-the-curtain capacity at the Comédie Française went as high as some 340 persons (230 or more on the stage proper, 108 in the stage boxes). Indeed, at capacity, there were more spectators paying premium prices behind the the curtain than there were in front of it. Taking the 230 stage seat spectators, plus 36 in the first tier of stage boxes, one obtains 266 admissions behind the curtain at the highest price, while out in the auditorium only 200 such places were available, of which 160 were in the lower boxes and 40 were in the orchestra. Viewed another way, 340 admissions behind the curtain could bring in, at normal prices, nearly twice as much revenue as 700 admissions to the *parterre*. The ratio of revenue to spectator was thus almost exactly reversed for those two types of admission. And since it was surely more agreeable to put up with several hundred marquis than with twice as many of the rowdies who populated the *parterre*, it is not surprising that those who made their living from the theatre were reluctant to chase spectators from the stage.

The numbers of spectators on the public stages in Paris had thus evolved from the modest thirty-two or thirty-six present during Molière's time to the three hundred and more in evidence starting with the Régence. This tenfold increase in the number of bodies to be contended with on the stage at peak times was not, of course, accompanied by any corresponding increase in available space. The problem of keeping order on the stage thus grew ever more difficult.

5

Keeping Order on the Stage

With so many spectators viewing the performance from behind the curtain, the problem of keeping order on the stage was nearly insurmountable. The most difficult task was to try to prevent unauthorized spectators from reaching the stage in the first place. This meant that personnel manning the ticket windows had to be discouraged from selling more stage tickets than there were places on the stage. It also meant that the *ouvreuses* or usherettes had to be motivated to allow entry only to spectators possessing a proper ticket. In addition, aggressive individuals had to be prevented from just plain sneaking up on the stage. It was, moreover, necessary to control the spectators once they had been admitted to the stage, to prevent them from taking it over altogether. To these ends, a variety of means was employed: physical barriers, royal ordinances, in-house penalties and, at times, armed guards. This chapter describes the measures introduced over the years.

In Molière's time, no physical restraint had been employed at any Paris theatre to prevent the *petits marquis* who populated the stage from pressing closer for a better view of the spectacle, or from occasionally sauntering across the stage, or, indeed, as we have seen, from being mistaken for part of the official spectacle itself. The historian of theatre, Germain Bapst, opined that "in the middle of the great century, balustrades certainly did not exist either at the Hôtel de Bourgogne, nor at the Hôtel Guénégaud, nor at the Marais Theatre."[1] And, indeed, several contemporary illustrations bear out this opinion.

A 1662 engraving depicting a scene from Raymond Poisson's *Zig Zag*, a one-act comedy performed at the Hôtel de Bourgogne, shows several spectators sitting in chairs placed along the side of the stage, with no balustrade in evidence (see fig. 3). Nor is there a balustrade in a series of 1666 engravings by Le Pautre, also depicting the Hôtel de Bourgogne stage. These engravings, meant to illustrate the very successful *Noce de village* by Brécourt, show numerous spectators seated and standing on the stage quite near the actors, not confined behind a balustrade (see figs. 4, 5, 16, 17 and 18).[2] Another contemporary illustration, representing a scene from *Cinna*, probably at the Hôtel Guénégaud, depicts spectators seated on two-tiered benches *(gradins)* in

Figure 16.   Scene. *La Noce de village*
Hôtel de Bourgogne, 1666
(Bibliothèque Nationale, Cabinet des Estampes)

Figure 17.   Scene. *La Noce de village*
Hôtel de Bourgogne, 1666
(Bibliothèque Nationale, Cabinet des Estampes)

Figure 18.   Scene, *La Noce de village*
              Hôtel de Bourgogne, 1666
              (Bibliothèque Nationale, Cabinet des Estampes)

front of stage boxes, but still no balustrade (see figs. 19, 20 and 21).[3] Clearly, then, in Molière's time, acting troupes were not yet thinking in terms of physical means to confine the spectators who had become a permanent part of the stage environment.

Nor would it seem that the idea was seriously considered until the Comédie Française built its new theatre on the rue des Fossés-Saint-Germain-des-Prés, and then only at the last minute. The troupe had not, at the outset, envisaged a balustrade for their new stage. A contractor's plan of the lower box level *(premières loges)* of the theatre drawn up by the architect François d'Orbay, and approved by La Grange, Le Comte and Raisin on April 14, 1688 (that is, one year before the opening of the new theatre), does not include any indication of a balustrade.[4] Preoccupied with what had turned into protracted and arduous negotiations relative to their new quarters, the troupe had had to address itself to matters more pressing than that of the *petits marquis*.

However, two weeks prior to opening night, the troupe turned its attention to that problem as well. On Saturday, April 2, 1689, the company held a special meeting to act on the matter.[5] A legal document was drawn up reflecting the decision to have a balustrade installed on either side of the stage. The *procuration*, in typical official run-on style, reads as follows:

> Today Saturday the second of April 1689 the company met in extraordinary session in its theatre to deliberate about the balustrade that they wish to have made for the new stage and after having counted all the votes resolved to have it made and for that purpose named Messrs Du Perier, D'Auvilliers, and Poisson, who together will do their best to have it installed by opening day of the new theatre they at the same time undertook a green melton carpet which will cover the area within the balustrade only and the company authorized them to enter into all necessary contracts without the balustrade preventing the opening [of the theatre] in case it is not completed....[see fig. 23].[6]

An agreement *(marché)* was drawn up that very day with Nicolas Tartarin, a master ironsmith, to construct and install the wrought iron balustrade (fig. 24). The terms of the contract made clear the kind of solid restraint the troupe had in mind for the *petits marquis*. The ironsmith, who agreed to accomplish the work before the opening date, subject to penalty, undertook to furnish

> approximately ten *toises*[7] of balustrade filled in with panels of wrought iron...installed on the stage of the theatre...in the rue des Fossés-Saint-Germain-des-Prés, with screw bolts passing through the theatre boards to hold them stable on the aforementioned stage, and good supports to keep them attached and solid...so they cannot be wobbly, and even to render the two sides of the first wing flats of the aforementioned stage open and moving in order for them to close and open as desired...the balustrades will be placed and installed on the aforementioned stage within the aforementioned time of the next fortnight, failing which...the aforementioned Tartarin consents that the price of the present contract will be diminished by the sum of one hundred *livres*....

Figure 19.   Allegory of *La Poesie*
              Perrault, *Le Cabinet des beaux-arts*
              (Bibliothèque Nationale)

Alexandre jnuenit et Pinxit

LA POESIE.

P. le Pautre delineauit et fecit

Figure 20.   Detail, Scene from *Cinna*
              Perrault, *Le Cabinet des beaux-arts*
              (Bibliothèque Nationale)

Melpomene

Cette muse majestueuse ne s'occupe qu'à représenter des sujets tragiques et c'est pour cela qu'on lui met un poignard en main avec des Sceptres et des couronnes.

4.

Figure 21.   Portrait of Melpomène
              H. Bonnart
              (Bibliothèque Nationale, Cabinet des Estampes)

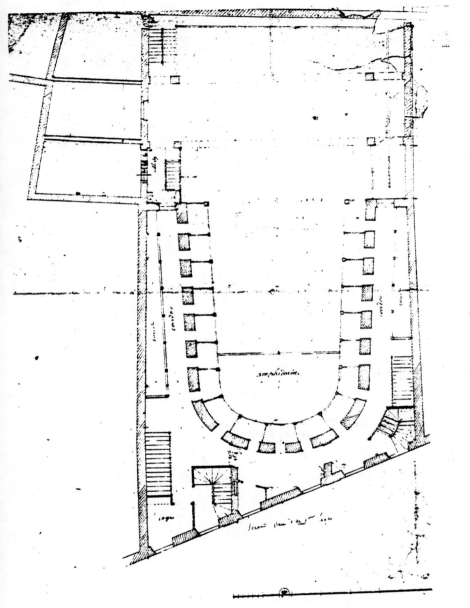

Figure 22.   Unidentified Plan, Comédie Française
Topographie de Paris
(Bibliothèque Nationale, Cabinet des Estampes)

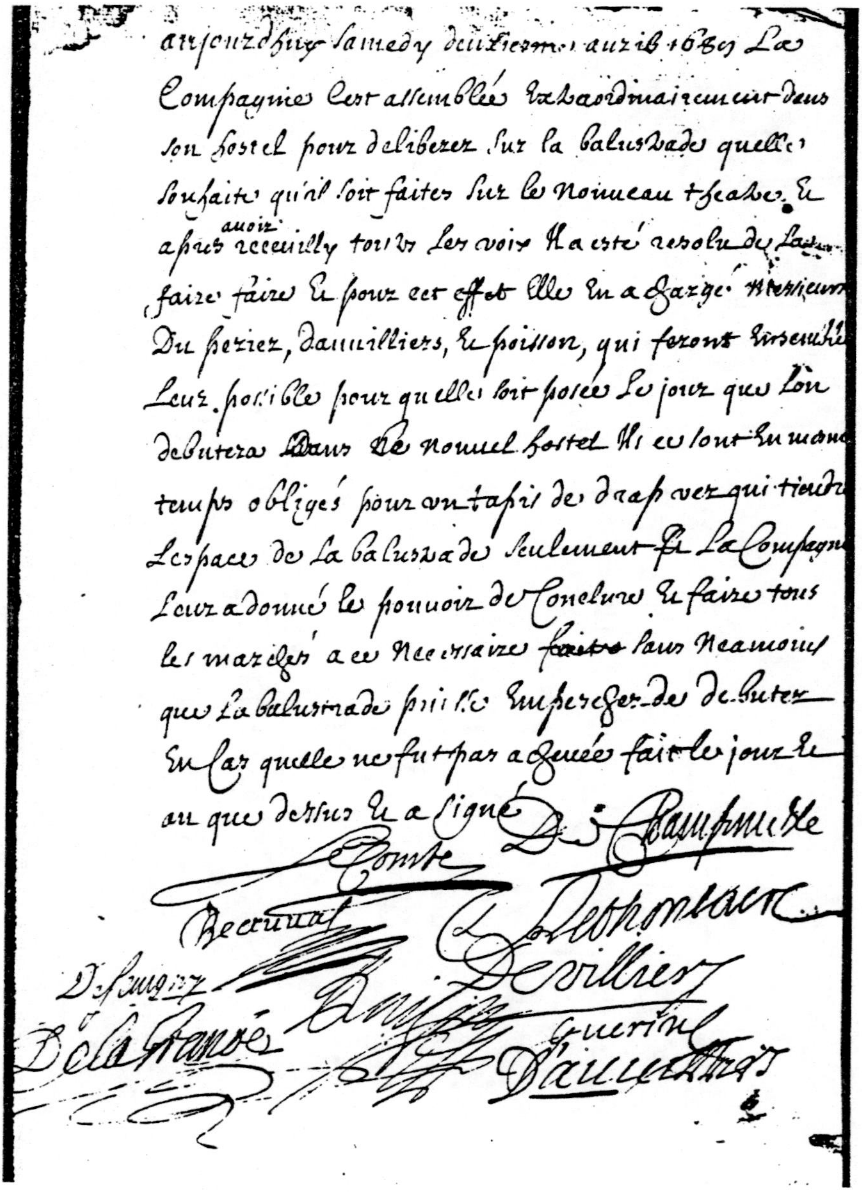

aujourdhuy samedy deuxiesme auril 1689 La
Compagnie s'est assemblée extraordinairement dans
son hostel pour deliberer sur la balustrade quelle
souhaite qu'il soit faite sur le nouueau theatre Et
après auoir recueilly tous les voix Il a esté resolu de la
faire faire Et pour cet effet Elle en a chargé Messieurs
Du periez, dauuilliers, Et poisson, qui feront ensemble
leur possible pour quelle soit posée Le jour que l'on
debutera dans Le nouuel hostel Ils en sont en mesme
temps obligés pour un tapis de drap vert qui tiendra
L'espace de la balustrade seulement Et La Compagnie
leur a donné le pouuoir de Conclure Et faire tous
les marchés a ce Necessaire sans Neamoins
que la balustrade puisse Empescher de debuter
En cas quelle ne fut pas achevée faite le jour et
an que dessus Et a signé

Baron

Comte

Becruual

Desauigny

Delagrange

Devilliers

Guerin

Dauuilliers

Figure 23. Procuration Ordering a Balustrade, Comédie
Française, 1689
(Archives Nationales, Minutier Central)

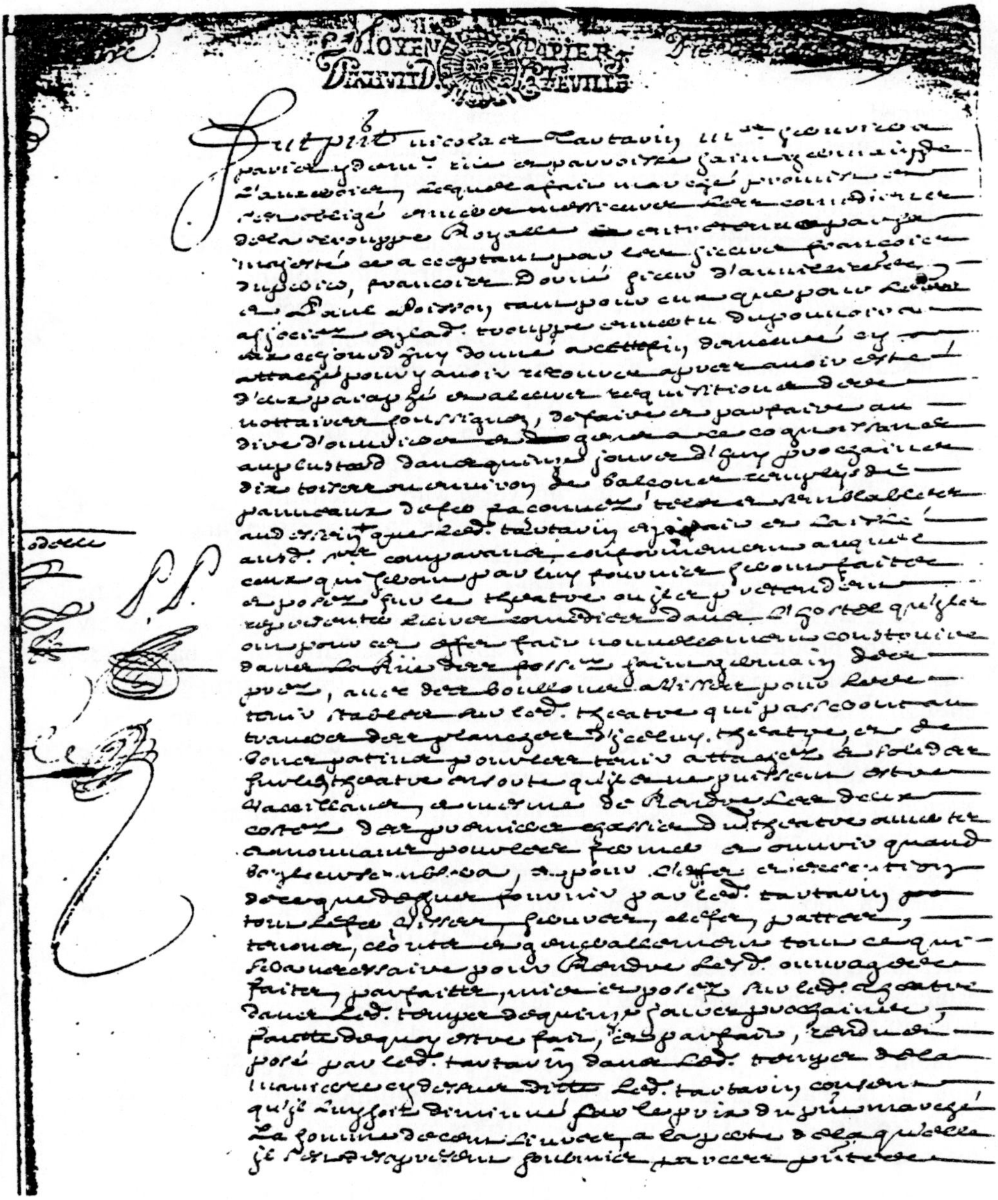

Figure 24. Excerpt, Contract for a Balustrade, Comédie
Française, 1689
(Archives Nationales, Minutier Central)

The notarized receipt signed by Tartarin indicates neither bonus nor penalty, so the balustrade was presumably successfully installed by the April 18, 1689 opening.

Further information about the balustrade at the Ancienne Comédie is recorded in a special account book kept by La Grange, and devoted to expenditures for the new theatre.[8] That document, kept in the actor's usual meticulous manner, indicates that the balustrade was beautified with gilded pommels atop the railing (see fig. 6), and that the benches and floor within its enclosure were covered with green melton fabric. Seventeen *aulnes* of *drap vert* were purchased for the benches, and twenty-three more for the floor covering *(tapis)*. (An *aulne* or *aune* is the equivalent of forty-six inches or 1.182 meters.) The cost of what came to be called the *enceinte de la balustrade*, that is, the area enclosed by the balustrades and set aside for spectators, was not trivial. The troupe spent a total of 801 £ 7s on this order-keeping stratagem, which amounted to about four percent of the approximately 200,000-*livres* cost of the new theatre. A little over half of the sum for the balustrade area was paid out to Nicolas Tartarin for the wrought iron work, with the remainder going for the golden pommels, the green fabric, miscellaneous hardware items and a catered meal for some workers and the stage decorator.

While the presence of balustrades on the stage of the new Comédie Française was surely helpful in keeping spectators in check, it did not entirely resolve the problem posed by the *petits marquis*. Installation of the balustrade was only symptomatic of what was to become a continuing struggle. Eager enough to be admitted to the stage, this segment of the audience was not always willing to pay for the privilege. Remedial procedures were established at the troupe's April 12, 1695 meeting. The minutes instruct that an employee "will be stationed on the stage in the best manner to prevent anyone from entering the stage who has not paid for the stage."[9]

Besides unauthorized freeloaders, the troupe had to contend with gentlemen who were willing to pay, but who had arrived at the theatre after the stage tickets had been sold out. Certain of those could be particularly determined and resourceful in gaining access to the stage. From some bylaws established by the troupe in 1697, we learn that such latecomers had been in the habit of taking a circuitous route which allowed them to circumvent theatre personnel. By using the little passageways or *petites cours* running on either side of the main corridors (labeled "N" on the Blondel plan of the *rez de chaussée*, fig. 25) and leading to the latrines at ground level, patrons could reach a small staircase ("S") whose purpose was communication between the stage and the orchestra pit. At the same time, however, it allowed one to pass from ground level to stage level, which was precisely what the *petits marquis* without proper tickets desired to accomplish. That pathway, it was resolved,

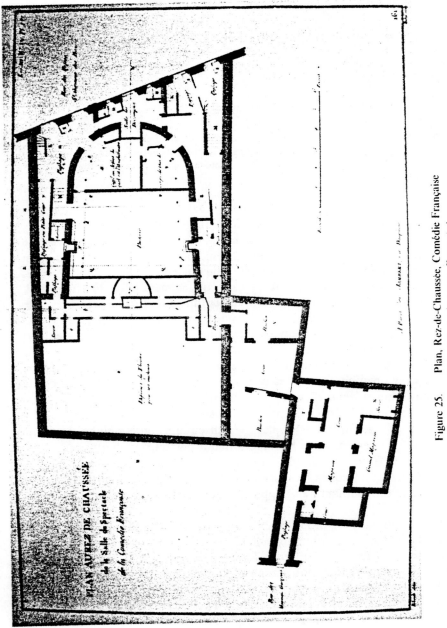

Figure 25.   Plan, Rez-de-Chaussée, Comédie Française
(Blondel, *Architecture Française*)

would be blocked by installation of a heavy partition at the bottom of the staircase in question. As set forth by the bylaws:

> At the bottom of the little staircase, where the door leading below stage is located, a heavy partition will be constructed to prevent the possibility of surprise entry to the green-rooms and to the stage by way of the little courtyard, as has happened several times, this violation not being preventable by any other means.[10]

The same set of bylaws reminded personnel that:

> The usherette at the entrance to the stage will likewise not admit anyone without a proper ticket, except for persons included in the Stage List [of persons entitled to complimentary admission] and will not admit any children of actors or supernumeraries either, under any pretext whatever.[11]

The combat intensified the following year. The closing of the Comédie Italienne in May of 1697 rendered the Comédie Française essentially the only game in town, and caused pressures to mount. What Barbier would describe some years later as the "great number of nobles and young men . . . who often came onto the stage without having a seat" did not lessen.[12] Thus, early in 1698, a year during which attendance at the Comédie Française was to attain peak proportions,[13] the troupe found it necessary to introduce further measures. The balustrade as it had been designed and installed in 1689 was no longer effective. It was therefore decided, at the weekly meeting of January 20, 1698, to extend the balustrade and expand the seating within its enclosure.

It is not clear in just what manner the balustrade was lengthened, since the first two wing openings were already blocked. In any case, the minutes of the troupe's meeting reflect the frustration of its members: the balustrade was to be extended, they explain, "to prevent the confusion on stage of persons mingling with the actors performing the play, which circumstance obliterates all its beauty and so interferes with the actors that a perfected performance of the play becomes impossible." Poisson, who had sketched the proposed modifications for his colleagues during their meeting, was put in charge of the project. A royal ordinance in support of the changes was promulgated by Versailles.[14]

The task of keeping order on the stage was not limited to the problem of the *petits marquis*. Attention to behavior in the twelve boxes which were behind the curtain was also in order. Indeed, the privacy afforded by the stage boxes (as well as by the other boxes) was not necessarily an unmixed blessing. Shortly after moving to its new theatre, "the Company . . . found it appropriate to create a position for the inspection of what goes on . . . in the *balcons*, and in the first, second and third tiers of boxes." Several years later it was decided to eliminate the problem in the third tier of stage boxes, if nowhere else.

It was resolved that in the future neither actors nor actresses, supernumeraries nor domestics will be admitted to the third tier of stage boxes above the stage in order to avoid the indecencies that take place there every day and that the aforementioned stage boxes will henceforward be available only to customers paying 30 sous as in the second tier of boxes.[15]

In the meantime, a longer balustrade at the Comédie Française in 1698 had obviously not restored "beauty" and "perfection" to that theatre. Nor had the surveillant routinely in charge of maintaining order at the Comédie Française (each of the three theatres was assigned its own overseer) been of much help.[16] Two 1713 letters from Pontchartrain, secretary of domestic affairs to Louis XIV, suggest that the situation on the stage of the Comédie Française was as bad as, if not worse than, ever. Addressed to d'Argenson, the chief of police,[17] the first communication directs that a policeman be stationed on the stage itself. Pontchartrain feels that order can be enforced only "by expressly recommending to Rivière [a police officer] that he station himself on the stage of the Comédie." His job will be to observe "those who make noise or stand outside the balustrade," and to inform himself of "their names and titles."[18] Moreover, Pontchartrain sternly proclaims, the practice of distributing more stage tickets than there were places on the stage was to be stopped.

It is absolutely necessary that no more stage tickets be distributed than there is capacity inside the balustrades, for when those two areas are entirely filled, if more people arrive on the stage, it is necessary either to make them leave or to permit them to stand outside the balustrades.[19]

Mindful of social pressures, the royal secretary then observes that once spectators had gotten as far as the stage, "it would be rather harsh, and even impossible, to make them leave by force, particularly when they are persons of quality," such that "by stating at the door that the stage is full and that there are no more tickets, no one will have cause to complain."[20]

These admonishments were apparently not heeded to good effect, for several weeks later in a second letter, Pontchartrain exhorts the chief of police to continue "to keep his hand in." The only way to prevent the abuse from recommencing, he reiterates, "is to have Rivière stationed with a guard at the entrance to the stage, and to absolutely oblige the troupe to give out only as many stage tickets as there is room behind the balustrades."[21]

Keeping order on the stage was a continuing concern of the *lieutenant de police*. In a report written on April 25, 1714, he declares that: "I have learned that the balustrade at the Comédie conforms to the regulations we have prescribed and that scrupulous attention is being paid to not allowing anyone outside its boundaries."[22] However, as subsequent ordinances suggest, no measure proved effective for long. Stern words and armed guards notwithstanding, there continued to be "a large number of nobles and young men who often came onto the stage without having a seat."[23]

Nothing much had changed several decades later, when, in August of 1748, Voltaire himself asked for police assistance. Worried about the effect of too many stage spectators on the décor for his *Sémiramis* he wrote to Berryer, the lieutenant general of the police, "I beg of you, please, to order two officers stationed on the stage to keep back a crowd of young Frenchmen who are hardly made for an encounter with Babylonians."[24] Nor had thirty years improved the distribution of tickets, for Berryer answered that

> The abuse is due to the excessive number of tickets that the troupe distributes. Moreover, since stage tickets are not differentiated from other tickets for the best seats, everyone prefers the stage and wants to be there, for it is easier to communicate there than it is in the boxes; I have just instructed the officer to speak to the troupe on my behalf and to cooperate with them in taking appropriate precautions at the earliest opportunity so as not to admit more people than there should be to the stage.[25]

The way the stage must have looked with armed guards is suggested by a Cochin drawing depicting a 1745 performance of Voltaire and Rameau's *comédie-ballet La Princesse de Navarre* at Versailles (fig. 26). Two royal guards, one on each side, bear muskets, while four more carry lances. Several unarmed guards, arms outstretched, are attempting to hold back spectators pressing forward from the wings. Though not entirely comparable to the Comédie Française (this was a private royal stage with women spectators present on it) the general idea was the same.

The insistence and the stampede behavior of the *petits marquis* can be assessed not only in terms of the wear and tear on the nervous systems of those who tried to control it, but in terms of material wear and tear. The green melton *tapis* that covered the floor and the footrests *(marche-pieds)* within the enclosure of the balustrade seems to have been in frequent need of attention. Installed in 1689 at the same time as the balustrades, the floor covering was, according to the records, repaired or replaced every few years. The *feuille d'assemblée* for March 24, 1692 reports that "Mr. Le Comte and Mr. Du Perrier will take care of repairing the carpet cloth...and will buy some material if they need some for the carpet." Minutes for the March 21, 1695 assembly mention "a new carpet for the stage." On September 20, 1700, "It was ruled by the company that new footrest covering be made for the stage and Mr. Dancourt took on that task." An invoice dated March 10, 1718, lists three *livres* "for having twice repaired the carpeting," while a year later, the minutes for March 13, 1719 state that "the company has resolved...to buy green carpet cloth for the stage."[26]

It is not known whether, prior to their banishment from Paris in 1697, the Comédie Italienne had followed the example of their rivals by installing balustrades on the stage of the Hôtel de Bourgogne. It is quite clear, however, that once returned from exile in 1716, the troupe did from the very start have balustrades on its stage. The royal ordinance of May 18, 1716 permitting "the reestablishment of a new Troupe de Comédiens Italiens" contains a specific

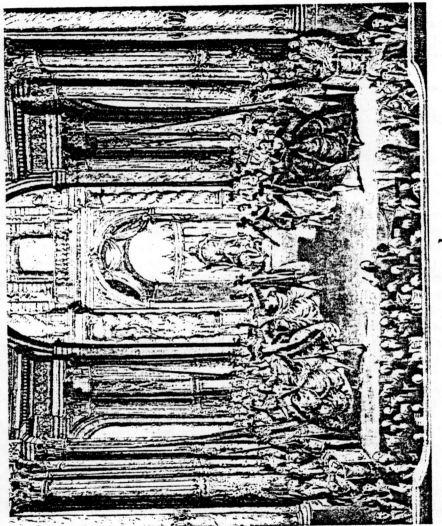

Figure 26.   Scene, *Princesse de Navarre*
             Versailles, 1745
             Drawing by Cochin, fils.
             (*Musée de l'Opéra*)

prohibition against spectators stopping "outside the area enclosed by the balustrades put there to keep the spectators seated, and separated from the actors."[27] The existence of balustrades at the Hôtel de Bourgogne is confirmed by a sketch made in 1717 by Sir James Thornhill, an English visitor who attended a performance at that theatre early in the year. A painter and set designer, Sir James used his professional eye to enter in his diary a rough drawing of what he saw (figs. 27 and 28).[28]

As at the Comédie Française, armed guards were stationed on the stage of the Comédie Italienne. An unfortunate accident arising from this practice and resulting in the wounding of an actor took place in February of 1759, just a year before spectators were removed from the stage of that theatre.

> On the 23rd, the troupe performed *la Servante maitresse,* for the benefit of Mr. Balletti, who, some time earlier, had had his thigh broken by a bullet in the play *Camille magicienne,* in which he played Lélio: [the mishap was caused by] one of the soldiers who was supposed to force the tower and who picked up...the gun belonging to the stage sentry, who had gone out to answer nature's call. One could judge by the box-office receipts how touched the public was by this accident.[29]

A welter of royal ordinances aimed at keeping order on the stage was issued regularly by the Regency and subsequently by the government of Louis XV. Numerous pronouncements, in one combination or another, prohibit spectators from standing in the wings, standing outside the areas enclosed by the balustrades, and/or entering the stage area without a ticket. Generally these ordinances start out by forbidding any spectator from entering a theatre without paying and, once inside, from committing any disorder or interrupting the actors. They then go on to address the problem of stage spectators in particular, typically in language like the following, excerpted from an ordinance issued on April 10, 1720.

> His Majesty...likewise forbids, under the same penalty, persons of whatever standing or rank, from stopping in the wings that serve as entrance to the stage of the Comédie, and [from standing] outside the area enclosed by the balustrades placed there to keep spectators seated and separated from the actors, so that the latter can give their performances with more decorum and to the greater satisfaction of the public.[30]

Such wording was designed to apply to the Comédie Française and, starting in 1716, to the Comédie Italienne. The Opéra and the theatres connected with the Foire Saint Laurent and the Foire Saint Germain were covered by similar ordinances. Their language, however, was modified to exclude mention of balustrades, a feature that not all of those theatres possessed. Such ordinances were issued frequently and regularly throughout the first half of the eighteenth century, as attested to by the many examples in the collections of both the Bibliothèque Historique de la Ville de Paris and the Bibliothèque Nationale.[31]

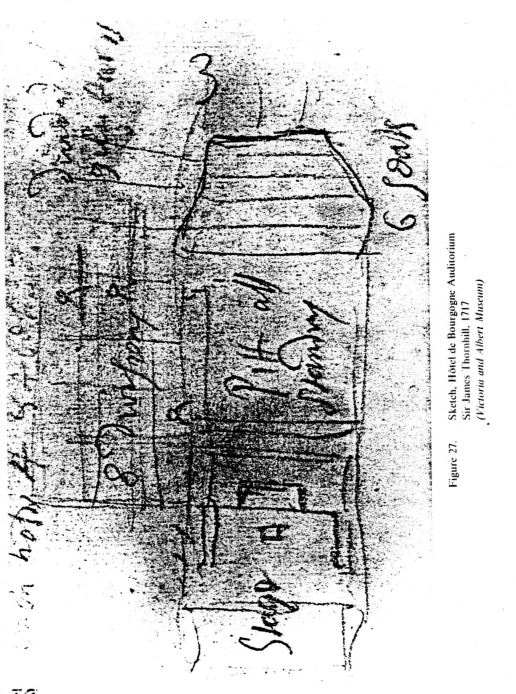

Figure 27. Sketch, Hôtel de Bourgogne Auditorium
Sir James Thornhill, 1717
(Victoria and Albert Museum)

52

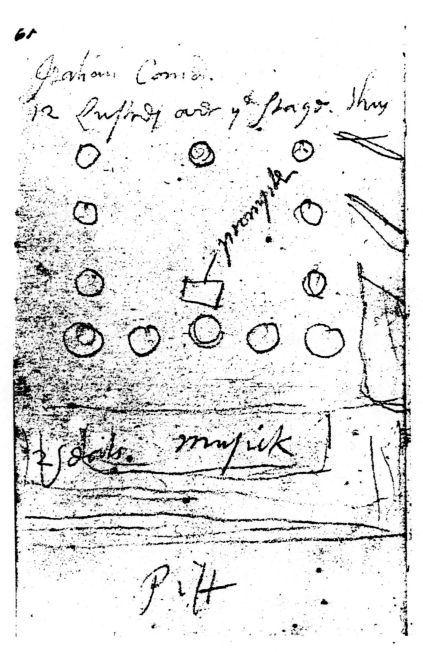

Figure 28.   Sketch, Hôtel de Bourgogne Stage
              Sir James Thornhill, 1717
              (Victoria and Albert Museum)

Indeed, so in the habit were royal bureaucracy and royal printers of issuing admonishments to spectators on the stage that they kept right on including them in ordinances about the theatre well after the practice of seating spectators there had been discontinued. Though spectators were banned from the stage of the Comédie Française in April of 1759, an ordinance promulgated eight months later, on December 12, 1759, once again exhorted his majesty's subjects not to stand outside the balustrades at that theatre.[32] The Comédie Italienne banned spectators from its stage the following year. Nonetheless, with somewhat surrealistic persistence, the same ordinance reappeared in 1769, nearly a decade after the last of the *petits marquis* had departed from the theatre boards of Paris![33]

A detailed picture thus emerges of the lengthy running battle over territorial rights to the Paris stage. The combatants were actors and their royal patrons on the one hand, and the ever-growing hordes of petty nobility on the other. Lingering in the wings, gaining access to the stage via little passageways, possessing a ticket or not, sitting or standing, within the confines of the balustrades or without, the *petits marquis* were determined to occupy the stage. Keeping order as best they could, actors and officials continued to fight an uphill battle for several more decades. Eventually, however, the phenomenon ran its course, and the *petits marquis* were banished from the Paris stage.

6

Removal of the Spectators from the Stage

As the eighteenth century progressed, a new theatrical aesthetic emerged, and as the move towards realism grew more compelling, the presence of spectators on the stage grew less tolerable. Thanks largely to the propaganda of Voltaire, and the financial assistance of an obscure benefactor, the Comte de Lauraguais, spectators were finally removed from the stage of the Comédie Française in 1759. The *petits marquis* had, in fact, already been chased from the stage of the Opéra a half century earlier for somewhat different aesthetic reasons. While not a great deal is known about what transpired at the Opéra near the end of the seventeenth century, the propaganda and protest campaign which occurred during the first part of the next century is well documented. It is also clear that the ensuing reform at the Comédie Française resulted in dramatic physical changes for the better both on the stage and in the auditorium.

The Opéra

The Opéra was the first of the three official theatres to get rid of spectators on the stage. With the demise of machine plays at the Comédie Française, the Opéra had become virtually the sole purveyor of *grand spectacle,* and so could not tolerate impediments to elaborate settings and machinery. In 1695 Du Tralage had already called for a royal ordinance to end this custom at the Opéra. "Once the king has expressed himself on the matter by providing a guard who would admit no one except the actors and those who serve them," he wrote, "the noblemen would be constrained to obey."[1] And, in fact, it would seem that such an ordinance was not long in being promulgated. The *Gazette de Rotterdam* for March 7, 1697 reports that "The King has forbidden Mr. Francine to allow anyone to be placed on the stage of the Opéra, which circumstance is causing it great loss. It is believed that this prohibition resulted from the complaint of one of the principal singers, Mr. du Mesnil, that he was mistreated by one of the individuals on the stage."[2]

This ordinance may not have been entirely effective in keeping spectators off the stage, because in 1732 another royal order stipulated that "in the future no person, regardless of title or rank, will be admitted to the stage of the Opéra, except for persons having rented a box whose entrance is from the stage. . . . "[3] In any case, one or another of these ordinances must have produced the desired effect, for Luigi Riccoboni, writing in 1738, states that "there are no more spectators on the stage of the Opéra, because the decorations, the machines, the choruses, and the dancers are already cramped. . . ."[4] And in 1754, the architectural historian Blondel, deploring the presence of stage seats at the Comédie Française and the Comédie Italienne, lauds the Opéra for the absence of same.[5]

Propaganda and Protest

Reform at the Opéra seems not to have had the least influence on the other two theatres, where the practice continued unchecked until after the middle of the century. As we have seen, sentiment had been building for decades in favor of removing spectators from the stage. Trenchant satire of the *petits marquis* who populated the theatre boards had found its way into literature. Wry anecdotes abounded, and neither royal ordinances nor official exhortations were wanting. What was lacking, however, was a powerful voice around which the theatre world could rally. Voltaire was that voice. Voltaire's earliest salvo directed at spectators on the stage was fired in 1730. In his *Discours sur la tragédie* which appeared as a companion piece to *Brutus*, he writes:

> The surroundings in which our plays are given, and the abuses which have crept in, are another cause of the coldness with which some theatre can be reproached. The benches meant for spectators on the stage constrict the stage and render any action almost unfeasible. They are why the stage decoration . . . is rarely suited to the play. Most of all, the benches are in the way of actors passing from one room to another before the spectator's eyes [which would] maintain both unity of place and verisimilitude.[6]

Having thus defined the crucial problem created by this practice, namely the severe impediment of both physical action and stage decoration, hence the virtual impossibility of stage realism, Voltaire lost few opportunities thereafter to campaign for reform. As the *Spectacles de Paris* observed, "M. de Voltaire had so acutely felt the need of a more spacious stage, that there are not many of his prefaces in which he fails to bring the matter up."[7]

The problem was brought home to Voltaire in even more immediate fashion upon production of his *Sémiramis* at the Comédie Française in 1748. Hoping by means of this tragedy to establish clear superiority over his rival Crébillon, Voltaire relied heavily on the visual element. The most spectacular of his plays so far, *Sémiramis* was to feature tableaux, supernatural appearances, and several changes of scenery, not to mention thunder, lightning and Greek costumes. A five-thousand-*livres* contribution from the king subsidized creation of the new sets, which were designed to occupy a portion of the area normally given over to stage seating. Since normal entry to the stage benches through the first two wings was blocked, it was necessary to construct a special entrance through the first tier of stage boxes (fig. 29).[8]

Voltaire had doubtless been hoping that this expanded décor would minimize the presence of the *petits marquis*. However, this did not happen. Over eleven hundred persons attended the first performance of *Sémiramis* (a record for the season), and the problem of too many stage spectators remained as bothersome as ever. Marmontel reports:

> The stage area was constricted by a crowd of spectators, some seated on the benches, others standing at the back of the stage and along the wings, such that the distraught Semiramis, as well as the ghost of Ninus leaving his tomb, were obliged to traverse a thick hedgerow of *petits-maîtres*. This indecency cast ridicule on the serious theatrical action.[9]

Indeed, according to the *Journal Encyclopédique*, the crowd on stage was so great that when, in Act III, the Hamlet-inspired ghost made its appearance, a voice cried, "Make way for the ghost," to the great amusement of the spectators.[10] Ruefully Voltaire reiterated his complaint.

> One of the greatest obstacles standing in the way of any important or touching action in our theatres is the crowd of spectators mixed in on the stage with the actors: this indecency was particularly felt during the first performance of *Sémiramis*. London's leading actress, present at that performance, couldn't get over her astonishment: she could not conceive how men could be so inimical to their pleasure as to spoil the spectacle rather than enjoy it.[11]

It would seem, moreover, that the stage decoration that did initially cover a portion of the *banquette* area was almost immediately withdrawn. Collé specifies that this new decoration was present "at the first two performances," thus implying that it was absent thereafter.[12] It is possible that following the second performance the extra scenery was retracted in exchange for clearing the spectators from the back of the stage, for, in the *Dissertation* accompanying publication of his tragedy, Voltaire wrote that "that abuse [excessive spectators on the stage] was corrected in subsequent performances of *Sémiramis*."[13]

Two years later in 1750, upon performance of *Oreste*, a play which continued Voltaire's campaign to crush Crébillon, the presence of stage spectators was, of course, just as damaging as ever. The *Mercure* reports that the tragic and theatrical qualities of Voltaire's new play were effectively undermined by "the ill-conceived arrangement of our stage, and the obtrusive and tumultuous crowd of young men conversing with one another, often without regard for anything other than capturing the attention of the

Figure 29. First Performance, *Sémiramis*
Comédie Française, 1748
Drawing by Saint-Aubin
(Decugis, *Le Décor de théâtre en France*)

spectators." How, the *Mercure* wonders, can it be expected that pathetic cries "which would be so touching, so penetrating against a background of silence, might rise above the noisy outbursts of glittering and inattentive youth, who hardly deign to let the actors slip through to the tiny part of the stage grudgingly left them, but where they should, nevertheless, be all alone."[14] The *petits marquis* were clearly still in top form.

Despite the complaints of Voltaire, the *Mercure* and others, an attempt, albeit abortive, was made not long afterward to cram still more spectators behind the curtain of the Comédie Française. During the Easter recess of 1751, additional stage boxes were built into the first wing space on either side of the stage.[15] Stacked three high and referred to as *petites loges*, the new seating constituted an extension of the stage boxes or *balcons* that were already there. Their configuration was probably similar to that of the *petites loges* shown on a later plan of the Comédie Italienne (fig. 38). Each *petite loge* was to hold four spectators, thus augmenting permanent seating on the stage by twenty-four places. Similar to an arrangement already in existence at the Opéra (fig. 30),[16] these *petites loges* were to be private, and rented on a yearly basis. Their installation at the Comédie Française was undertaken by the actor and author Sauvé-Delanoue, who had obtained oral approval from the king's Grand Falconer, M. de la Vallière.

Such new and privileged seating was meant to accommodate the elite, who, according to one commentator, wished to avoid being "under the gaze of the public," but who desired at the same time to remain "on the stage in closest possible proximity to the actors and actresses."[17] Indeed, one box had already been reserved by no less a personage than the Duc de Chartres, and another by M. de la Vallière himself. However, despite such illustrious patronage, the *petits loges* were ordered torn down by the Gentlemen of the King's Bed Chamber, who exercised complete and sometimes capricious control over Paris theatre. The Maréchal de Richelieu, First Gentleman, apparently motivated by a political grudge against one of the subscribers, joined forces with the other Gentlemen, offended at not having been consulted. They decreed removal of the new seating, an order which was carried out in the wee hours of the morning of April 26, 1751, opening day of the new season. Sauvé-Delanoue's reward for his initiative was seventeen days in Fort-l'Evèque prison. The installation of *petites loges* on the stage of the Comédie Française was not to take place until several years later.[18]

An idea of how these little boxes were situated, jammed into any available space, can be obtained from one of Gabriel de Saint-Aubin's illustrations of the festivities in honor of Voltaire in 1778 (fig. 31). Depicting the Tuileries Theatre, at that time the home of the Comédie Française, the drawing shows the space between the two columns of the proscenium arch filled with three *petites loges*.

Figure 30.   Detail. Plan of the Opéra
              Legend superimposed
              (Dumont, *Parallèle des plans*)

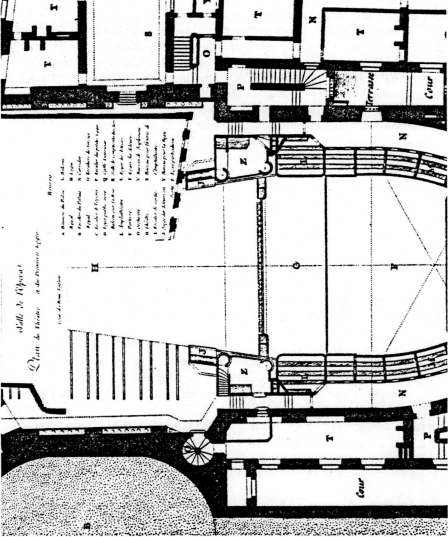

Figure 31.   Couronnement de Voltaire
Tuileries Theatre, 1778
(Musée du Louvre)

In the meantime, others of importance besides Voltaire were voicing their opposition to the presence of *petits-maîtres* on the stage. Deschamps, in defense of his 1739 play, *Médus*, attributed the failure of Persès's death scene to the crowding of spectators on the stage: "There was supposed to be a lot of space between Perseus and Medusa, but it was not possible for the actors to keep the necessary distance because of the large number of spectators on the stage."[19] Diderot took up the cause in 1758. In his familiar 1758 letter to Mme Riccoboni, he wrote:

> It seems to me . . . that you excuse the vice of our theatrical action because of the vice of our theatres. But wouldn't it be better to recognize that our theatres are ridiculous; that as long as they remain so the stage will be encumbered with spectators, our stage decoration will be false, and our dramatic action bad? We can't decorate the back of the stage, because there are people on the stage. What there should be is a stage empty of people, and full of decoration.[20]

De Belloy plaintively echoed this sentiment several months later upon the failure of his new play, *Titus*. Responding to the criticism that his play was marred by, among other things, an overly lengthy speech by Annius, De Belloy pointed out that the passage was only thirty lines long, but that the stage was so full of spectators that the audience could not tell that Annius was addressing the Senate and mistook the speech for an elaborate personal compliment which should have been much shorter.[21] In general, authors and critics alike agreed that the removal of spectators from the acting surface was long overdue.

Indeed, within the professional theatre world, the only real opposition to this idea came from the actors and actresses themselves. Save for the reform-minded Lekain, whose vision extended beyond the cash-box, the members of the Comédie Française were, understandably, most reluctant to undertake a change that would result in permanent elimination of revenue from 140 or more lucrative seats.[22] In all likelihood, Voltaire and the others would have advocated this reform in vain had not a benefactor come to the rescue.

Reform at the Comédie Française

Help appeared in the person of the Comte de Lauraguais, a former military man who had taken up letters. A hanger-on at the Comédie Française, he fancied himself a playwright, and proposed a generous, if perhaps not wholly disinterested, solution to the problem. Interested in several of the actresses at the Comédie, and no doubt even more interested in obtaining performance of two of his plays calling for elaborate productions,[23] Lauraguais had, early in 1759, come to the troupe with a plan. Assisted by Lekain, he had drawn up a proposal for remodeling the theatre so as largely to compensate for the loss of seating on the stage. He also volunteered to defray out of his own pocket the necessary remodeling costs, an expenditure that would have been out of the question for the impecunious Comédie Française to undertake alone.

At the same time, the thirty-year-old Lekain, who was probably the immediate motivating force behind the Comte de Lauraguais' offer, and who did not trust his older colleagues to accept the offer (he disdainfully referred to them as *la vétérance*), took action independently. Wishing to appeal directly to higher authority, Lekain sent to the minister in charge a plea entitled "Memorandum Tending to Prove the Need to Eliminate Benches from the Stage of the Comédie Française, Thereby Separating the Actors from the Spectators."[24] Dated January 29, 1759, the memorandum was accompanied by a plan view of the proposed changes. Lekain's argument takes several tacks. As usual, the ridiculousness of the custom is evoked: "Doesn't it seem . . . like the ultimate absurdity to watch the fathers of Greece and Rome appearing on our stage alongside young colonels, elegant senators, opulent financiers, and their richest intendants?" Those opposed to change are taunted: "At the mention of the word *reform*, welcomed by a modern actor [presumably Lekain himself] the veterans, enemy of anything new, will no doubt protest: *That everything has been just fine so far. . . .* " Lekain further suggests that those opposed fear exposure: "if they have some flaw, it is easier for them to conceal it in the twilight than to correct it in the light of day." Finally, he talks of the creative avenues that termination of this practice might open to decorators, stage engineers, theatre architects, authors and most of all to actors themselves who, "on a new stage" would find "a new career with room to exercise their imagination."

The actors ultimately approved the Lekain-Lauraguais plan, and Lauraguais undertook to contribute the cost of remodeling. Though initially estimated by the contractor at twelve thousand *livres*, it is not clear what the final bill for the needed work amounted to. No account books or bills have come down to us, but it is certain that the Comte de Lauraguais ended up spending much more than he had bargained for, probably in the neighborhood of sixty thousand *livres*, if Talma's account is accurate.[25] In any case, the project was scheduled for the Easter recess of 1759.

The Comédie Française announced the pending reform at its March 31 performance, the last before the recess. As was the practice, a relatively new troupe member, in this case Brizard, was designated to deliver the closing speech. He announced the projected innovation in these ingratiating terms:

> Gentlemen, we are on the point of seeing illusion and majesty reestablished on this stage. A friend of the Arts and Letters has been kind enough to offer the means, and our Superiors have given us permission to fulfill his vision, of a French stage shaped and arranged in more appropriate fashion. But until now, Gentlemen, thrown back upon our own resources, and obliged to employ our feeble talent to create realistic-seeming spectacles which everything contrived to destroy, we have sorely tried your indulgence! Your indulgence has not flagged nor failed, and you have always granted it, mindful of the obstacles which we had to surmount.[26]

The closing program consisted of Chateaubrun's five-act verse tragedy, *Les Troyennes*, and *Le Double Veuvage*, a three-act prose comedy by Dufresny. Habitués of the stage seats appear to have come out in force to put in one last appearance, since receipts for that date were not only the highest of the year (3,957 *livres*), but higher than those of any closing performance for at least ten seasons.

Workers invaded the theatre immediately afterwards, and, under the general supervision of Lekain, began the rather complicated transformations that had to be executed during the three-week closing. According to the *Année littéraire*, "they worked day and night during the three weeks of vacation," and, indeed, significant changes were effected.[27]

Replacement of the Stage Seats

On the stage itself, all of the rows of benches, as well as both wrought iron balustrades were, of course, removed. At the same time, the capacity of the stage boxes *(balcons)* was increased. This was accomplished by eliminating, in the first tier, the partition between boxes in order to form one large box where before there had been two, and by crowding three rows of benches into the space meant for two. Thus, instead of two boxes side by side holding a total of eighteen people, one large box could hold from twenty-four to thirty (compare fig. 10 with figs. 32 and 33).[28] This arrangement does not seem to have been carried out in the second tier of *balcons* (the third had been converted to *petites loges* in 1757), because starting in 1759 the registers show rental of *balcons* for thirty-six *livres*, which would represent a box with a seating capacity of six. This suggests that perhaps the second level was redivided to form three, or possibly even four, boxes with six places each (see fig. 34). This rearrangement increased the total seating capacity of the first two tiers of stage boxes from 72 to perhaps as many as 128.

At the same time, additional seating was established very close to the stage in an area newly designated as the *parquet*. This new seating was created by taking over the entire orchestra pit, as well as a portion of the *parterre* (standees' pit). According to Barbier, the *parquet* could hold over 180 spectators. "They took away from the *parterre* to form a *parquet*, which holds more than one hundred eighty persons; apart from the orchestra, they made the amphitheatre smaller in order to lengthen the *parterre*."[29] Barbier's account, written in 1759, does not correspond exactly to any of the three extant plans of the Comédie Française which subsequently appeared, the *Encyclopédie* plan (1772), the Dumont *Parallèle* plan (1774) and the Roubo plan (1777). The date each plan was actually drawn is not known, but it should be borne in mind that the Comédie Française moved to the Tuileries Theatre in 1772. In any case, none shows as much *parquet* seating as described by Barbier, but the Dumont

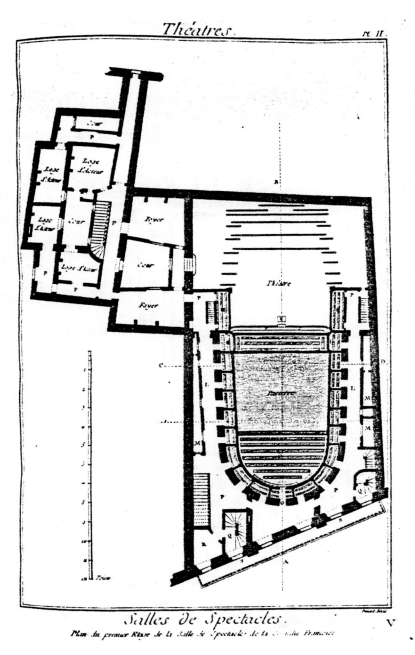

Salles de Spectacles.

Plan du premier Etage de la Salle de Spectacle de la Comédie Française.

Figure 32.   Plan, Premier Etage, Comédie Française
             (Encyclopédie)

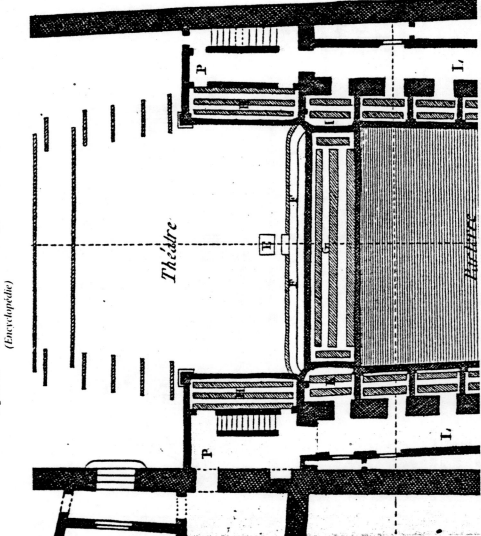

Figure 33.   Detail, Plan, Premier Etage, Comédie Française
(*Encyclopédie*)

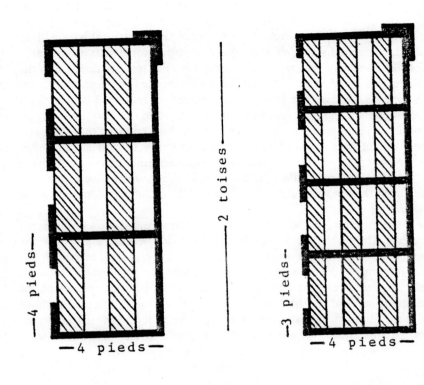

Three boxes
seating
six persons
each

Four boxes
seating
six persons
each

Figure 34.   Hypothetical Plans, Second Level *Balcons*,
               Comédie Française
               After 1759

plan comes closest. From the plan in the *Encyclopédie* (fig. 32) we can see how the three short rows of lateral benches which already existed at either side of the orchestra pit before 1759 were extended all the way across the center at the expense of the pit itself. But the plan does not show the placement of additional benches in the *parterre*, nor does it show contraction of the amphitheatre as mentioned by Barbier. As shown in the *Encyclopédie*, the three benches running across the *orchestre* were four *toises* in length. (A *toise*, it will be remembered, contained six *pieds*, and a *pied* measured somewhat more than a foot: about 12.8 inches). Assuming four seats per *toise* (as was the case in the boxes), there would have been 16 seats per bench, hence forty-eight places for the three benches. Adding the two or three places on each side bench, there were, according to the *Encyclopédie* plan, fifty-two to fifty-four places altogether in what was formerly the *orchestre*. To arrive at the 180 seats mentioned by Barbier, it would have been necessary to add six or seven additional rows of benches in the *parterre*, an arrangement that would have been entirely feasible, particularly if a corresponding number were removed from the amphitheatre. The Roubo plan (fig. 35) is almost identical to the *Encyclopédie* plan.

The Dumont plan (fig. 36), on the other hand, shows six rows of benches in the *parquet*. Unlike the *Encyclopédie*, no short side benches are shown: the lateral benches run across the entire available width. No scale is provided, but the legend informs us that the *parquet*, or *orchestre* as it is called by Dumont, measured 29 *pieds* from side to side. Again assuming that one spectator occupied about one and one-half *pieds* (one-fourth of a *toise*), there would have been room for about twenty spectators per row. Subtracting the seating in the orchestra pit area shown (about eight places), there would have been room, according to this plan, for about 112 spectators in the *parquet*. The *parterre* is shown as starting after the second *loge* instead of after the first, but remaining about the same size, while the amphitheatre, with improved arrangement of benches, is reduced from eight rows to five.

The plans are not in agreement either in indicating how remodeling affected the placement of the musicians. The Dumont plan shows retention of a portion of the orchestra, plus creation of what appears to be additional space for musicians partially beneath the front edge of the stage. The *Encyclopédie* plan, on the other hand, indicates total elimination of the orchestra pit as shown on the Blondel plan, and relegation of the musicians to the long narrow space beneath the edge of the stage. This is in agreement with Roubo's 1777 statement that "the Orchestra or the place where the symphony is located, was separated from the *parquet* only by a partition, and had but a single bench running across the entire width of the stage." (Roubo, however, may have been basing his statement on the *Encyclopédie* plan alone, since by the time he wrote the Comédie Française had already moved to the Tuileries).[30] A single cramped

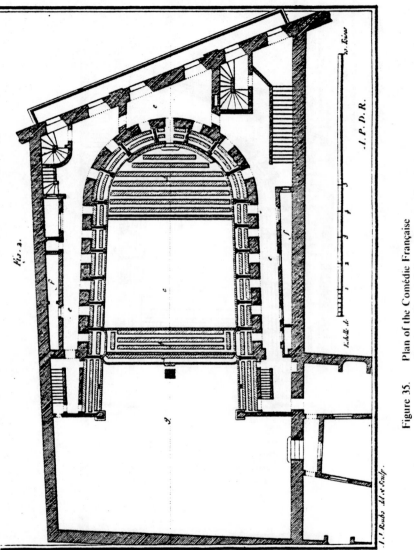

Figure 35.   Plan of the Comédie Française
(Roubou, *Traité de la construction des théâtres*)

Figure 36.   Plan of the Comédie Française
               (Dumont, *Parallèle des plans*)

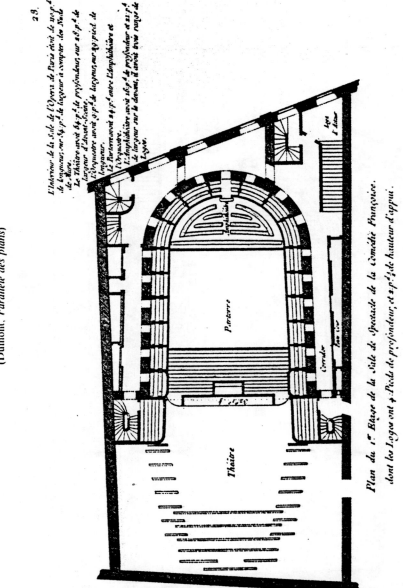

29.

L'Intérieur de la Sale de l'Opera de Paris étoit de 114. p.^{ds}
de longueur, sur 84. p.^{ds} de largeur à compter des Sieds
de Mure.
   Le Théatre avoit 84 p.^{ds} de profondeur, sur 28 p.^{ds} de
largeur d'Avant-Scene.
   L'Orquestre avoit 9. p.^{ds} de largeur, sur 49. Pieds de
longueur.
   Le Parterre avoit 24. p.^{ds} entre l'Amphithéatre et
l'Orquestre.
   L'Amphithéatre avoit 16.p.^{ds} de profondeur et 21.p.^{ds}
de largeur sur le devant, il avoit trois rangs de
Loges.

Théâtre

Parterre

Orquestre

Loges

Corridor

*Loges
d'Avant*

Plan du 1.er Étage de la Sale de Spectacle de la Comédie Françoise.
dont les Loges ont 4.Pieds de profondeur, et 2.p.^{ds} de hauteur d'appui.

bench for the musicians is not as unlikely as it seems, since the troupe was only entitled to a limited number of instruments.[31] The way such space for the musicians might have looked is suggested by the 1778 Saint-Aubin illustration referred to above (fig. 31).

In addition to the foregoing changes, three *loges grillées* (boxes screened by grillwork) were constructed underneath the *balcons* on either side of the stage. These new little boxes were partially submerged below stage level, looking out onto space formerly occupied by the stage benches. (The general appearance of *loges grillées* can be observed in figure 37, an illustration pertaining to the Comédie Italienne.) Access to the *loges grillées* was subterranean, and, like the *petites loges* which had been available since 1757, they were no doubt meant to appeal to those who desired complete privacy.[32] Also like the *petites loges*, the grilled boxes were probably rented, as a rule, on a long-term basis. In any case, when the theatre reopened in May, all three *loges grillées* on the king's side were leased for a two-year period to the Prince de Conti. The terms of the lease *(bail)* stipulated a quarterly rental fee of 1,250 *livres* for the triple box, and permitted its holder to undertake substantial remodeling. According to the language of the lease, "His Serene Highness will be entirely free to make ... whatever arrangement or modification he pleases to the site, provided it is not detrimental to the soundness of the auditorium, nor to its regular boxes." His Serene Highness was given further leave to make his four *pied* by six *pied* "emplacement" into "one or several compartments," either permanent, or with removable partitions, and was also permitted to convert the space beneath the staircase leading down to that area into "a large closet," provided that "an existing passageway which gave workers access to the area beneath the stage was left free." It is not difficult to imagine the cozy elegance offered by His Serene Highness's little hideaway.[33]

The price of the *loges grillées* appears to have been set to yield the equivalent of ten stage seats on either side of the stage.[34] Thus, when this replacement of the equivalent of twenty stage seats was added to the gain of seats in the stage boxes and the gain in the *parquet,* the actors were adequately, or more than adequately, compensated for the loss, of the 140 permanent places that were removed from the stage. Below in tabular form is a resumé of the results. As previously noted, there are significant discrepancies in the number of *parquet* seats indicated by the three available sources of information: Barbier, Dumont and the *Encyclopédie*. The number reported by Barbier probably comes closest to the truth, since it is unlikely that the *comédiens* would have settled for much less than parity, and since the plans seem not to have been drawn with great care (see note 30 to this chapter).

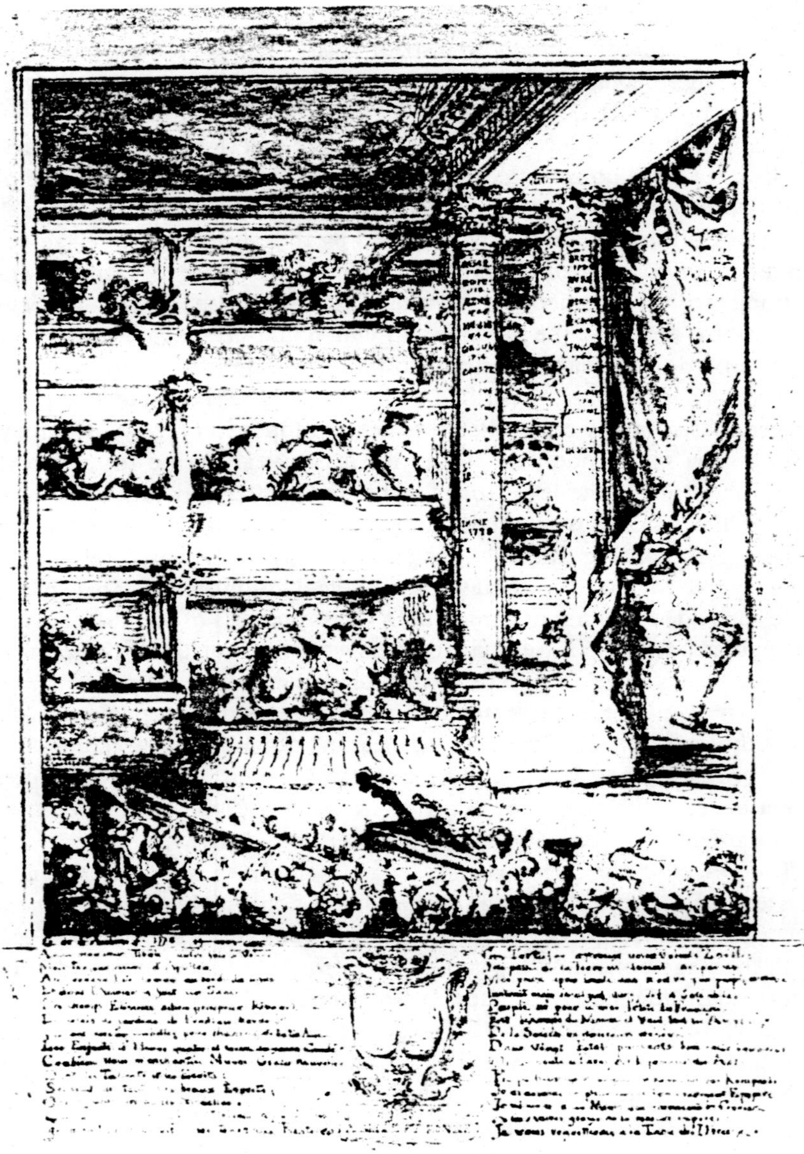

Figure 37.   A Performance at the Comédie Italienne
              Hôtel de Bourgogne, ca. 1772
              Drawing by P.A. Wille
              (Hennin Collection)

Table 2.   Seating Substitutions. 1759 Remodeling at the Comédie
Française

	Number of Seats Before Remodeling	Number of Seats After Remodeling
Permanent Stage Seats	140	0
Extra Benches	28	0
First *Balcon* Seats	36	48
Second *Balcon* Seats	36	48
Loges grillées (Equivalent Seats)	0	20
Orchestra/ *Parquet*	40	180
Total	280	296

The loss of or compensation for revenue from standing-room customers on the stage, whose main purpose in coming to the theatre was defeated, cannot, of course, be readily calculated. But as Barbier observes:

> It is true... that the troupe will lose at big performances, because a large number of nobles and young men came onto the stage, without having a seat, solely to see the general spectacle and the women in the boxes, and to be seen; to chat among themselves, come and go in the warming rooms, chat with the actresses—diversions and conveniences that they will not have when they take a stationary seat in the *parquet;* for the troupe, it meant that many six pound écus.[35]

On the whole, however, these substitutions must have worked out to be financially satisfactory because receipts for the succeeding period did not decline, but continued a general upward trend until the Revolution.[36]

In addition to compensating for the loss of stage seating, the remodeling resulted in two extremely important improvements. For one, the second wing, blocked off for so many decades by the rows of *banquettes* and by the balustrade, was now free to be used as intended, for actors' entrances and exits, and for stage decoration. (The first wing, it is important to note, was presumably still obstructed by the *petites loges* that had been constructed in 1757.) For another, the actual usable stage surface between the footlights and the third wing flats was now more than the double of what it had been with stage benches present. Where before this aperture had measured fifteen *pieds* at the front and eleven at the rear, now, with benches removed, these dimensions were more like thirty *pieds* and twenty-six *pieds* respectively[37] (compare figs. 10 and 33). That area of the stage was increased from approximately 260 square *pieds* to 560 square *pieds*.

Upon conclusion of the Easter recess, the remodeled Comédie Française began its new season. The debt of gratitude owed to the Comte de Lauraguais was publicly acknowledged by Brizard, who, having delivered the closing compliment three weeks earlier, was now called upon for the opening compliment. Speaking "in the name of the Comédiens Français," Brizard offered "public testimony of their gratitude to M. le Comte de Lauraguais, who was willing to undertake the expense of this remodeling of the stage, which all Paris applauded."[38] If the Comte de Lauraguais had indeed had ulterior motives for his generosity, his hopes were not satisfied. Gratitude notwithstanding, the only reward the Comédie Française ever accorded their benefactor was a free pass to their theatre.[39]

7

After the Reform

The removal of spectators from the stage of the Comédie Française was universally applauded by public, critics, and the theatre world alike. Reform had been eagerly awaited, and almost no one missed the opportunity to opine, by newsletter, by journal or in private correspondence; approbation was only rarely tempered by cautionary reflection. Undertaking a similar reform a year later, the Comédie Italienne profited from the occasion to effect a thorough remodeling of the old Hôtel de Bourgogne. However, much less of a fuss attended the transformations at that theatre, doubtless because the novelty was over. In any case, following the Easter recess of 1760, the *petits marquis* as an institution were at long last gone from all of the stages of Paris. But official reform did not mean total cessation of stage seating, for at benefit performances and on other special occasions, spectators were still to be seen occupying the stage. In the meantime, across the Channel, London theatre, no doubt taking note of the successful formula adopted in Paris, finally brought about its own reform in 1762.

Reactions to the Reform

The better to illustrate its accomplishment, the Comédie Française opened the 1759-60 season with a performance of *Les Troyennes (The Trojan Women)*, the same tragedy that had been featured at closing a few weeks earlier. The public was apparently interested in making the comparison: attendance at the March 31 closing performance was very high, and the first performance of the new season also drew a large number of customers to the best seats.[1] Reaction to the absence of the *petits marquis*, who had reigned so long on the stage of the Comédie Française, can only be termed ecstatic. Praise for this innovation appeared in all of the appropriate places. The *Année littéraire* was first:

> You see, Sir, it is always well to rise up courageously against abusive practices; sooner or later they are corrected; there has been so much talk and so much criticism of this one, that in the end the wishes of literate people and sensible spectators have been fulfilled.... The day after

Low Sunday, the opening of the new season, fashionable Paris saw, with a satisfaction I cannot express to you, our leading theatre, our theatre par excellence, just as everyone had been hoping to see it for so long, that is to say, delivered of that glittering and frivolous element of the public, at once its ornament and its embarrassment—those high-toned people, those officers, idle magistrates, and charming *petits-maîtres* who know everything without learning anything.... French frivolity will no longer stand in ridiculous contrast to Roman gravity. The Marquis de *** will no longer elbow Cato....[2]

The *Mercure de France,* evoking the sorry state of the national theatre prior to this reform, joined in.

The French theatre, richest of all theatres, not excepting those of Athens and Rome, degraded, through improper performance, the finest creations of genius in both dramatic genres. Precious truth...was lost in the tumultuous mingling of spectactors with actors. Augustus deliberated in the midst of our *petits-maîtres;* and...while Tartuffe verified whether anyone could surprise him seducing the wife of his friend, he was surrounded by a hundred witnesses of his tête-à-tête with her. One thought oneself accustomed to this shocking irregularity, but verisimilitude was nonetheless affected.... A still greater drawback was the difficulty of developing dramatic action. The playwright...felt his imagination constricted between two hedgerows of spectators who cut him off from two-thirds of the stage.[3]

Both periodicals found the new policy well illustrated by *Les Troyennes.* The *Mercure* reported that "the tragedy of *Les Troyennes,* with which the season opened, was seen at last with all the pageantry that it calls for," and the *Année littéraire* was particularly impressed with the dramatic effect of large numbers of Greek soldiers.

Indeed, there is a fine moment in this drama: it is when the Greek soldiers, commanded by Ulysses, go forward to destroy Hector's tomb under the very eyes of Andromaque. This scene always failed in previous performances; in this one it was executed with all the fire of truth; the movements of this large group, which gave the appearance of a considerable detachment, and which filled the empty space on the stage, presented in combination with Andromaque's desperate tears...wrought upon the enchanted public a legitimate impression of terror.[4]

Those who kept tabs on the theatre in private journals were equally enthusiastic about the reform. Barbier, in attendance on opening night, lauded the effect—shades of simultaneous décor!—of a stage that had room for more than a single setting (a desideratum Voltaire had earlier expressed in connection with his *Brutus).*

On Monday the 23rd, the day after Low Sunday, a performance was given on the new stage. Everyone was pleased with it, and there is no comparison. The stage, to which no one is now admitted, represents a room in a palace, as well as another location; the actors move freely and illusion is much better maintained.[5]

On the same theme, the *Mercure* suggested that perpetuation of unity of place had been largely a matter of coping with the presence of so many *petits-maîtres* on the stage, and that now the French stage was free of that undesirable constraint.

> One had to be resigned to conforming to unity of place: for if the playwright dared free himself from that rule, the stage refused the change he had promised himself.... Thus, all subject matter requiring alternating passage from one place to another, like that of *Coriolan, Régulus,* etc.... was unfeasible on the stage, short of mutilation.... Today...dramatic action is liberated from the unity of place that Aristotle prescribed, but to which the Greek poets themselves did not care to be subjected.[6]

Collé, who saw Rotrou's *Venceslas* a week later, felt not only that visual effect was enhanced, but that acoustics benefited as well.

> On Monday the 30th I went to see the auditorium of the Comédie Française, on whose stage no one is now tolerated, God willing that it lasts! It creates the best effect in the world: I even thought I noticed that the actors' voices are very much better heard. Theatrical illusion is now whole: one no longer sees Cesar on the point of wiping the powder off a fop seated in the front row of the stage, nor Mithridate expiring in the midst of people of our acquaintance; the ghost of Ninus bumping and elbowing a farmer-general, and Camille falling dead in the wings onto Marivaux and Saint-Foix, who move forward or back to be a party to the assassination [dodging] the blood which spurts out on them. This new form of theatre opens up a new career to authors of tragedy, giving them the possibility of incorporating spectacle, pageantry and more action into their poetry.[7]

Added to this chorus of relief and appreciation were a number of sanguine predictions for the future of French theatre. Actors, free to move about the stage, would at last be able to develop a more natural acting style; set-designers could produce more interesting, varied and realistic settings; authors could experiment. The *Correspondance littéraire* predicted salutary change in both décor and acting style.

> They have finally succeeded in banishing all the spectators from the stage of the Comédie Française, and in relegating them to the auditorium, where they should be. This move will not only oblige the actors to decorate their stage more suitably, but will bring about a revolution in stage play. When the actors are no longer constrained by spectators, they will no longer dare to arrange themselves in a circle like marionettes.[8]

That judgment was echoed and expanded upon by *Spectacles de Paris*, which felt that a stage cleared of spectators would act as a strong inspiration to playwrights.

> Playwrights, in outlining their works, will no longer be intimidated and chilled by the fear of inevitable mishap . . . due to a small stage and . . . the presence of spectators. There are equal advantages for the intelligent actor. Greater space will allow him to vary his posture, to change his position on the stage, to give more vivacity and naturalness to his gestures. In a word, the actor's genius will be able to interpret that of the poet; perhaps the force of theatrical illusion will even make the spectator forget both author and actor.[9]

In the midst of virtually universal praise of this reform, certain reservations were nonetheless expressed. It was feared by some that without the constraint of a very limited acting surface, the classical discipline of Corneille and Racine would be abandoned, in favor of extravagant action and spectacle. Fréron, for one, was apprehensive lest the Comédie Française become sidetracked by the special effects of "le merveilleux" (the supernatural) more appropriate to opera at the Palais Royal. "I am afraid that our dramatic poets might stray from the ancient rules . . . and abuse this enlargement of the stage to multiply tragic events, *coups de théâtre,* picturesque situations, daggers, tombs, ghosts, torches, battles, etc."[10] The *Mercure* acknowledged the existence of fears that "the ease of changing scenes might engage playwrights in extravagant compositions," but pointed out reassuringly that "there is no advantage which is not at times abused; and if authors stray, the sane part of the public will know how to lead them back."[11]

Nearly everyone, then, was enthusiastic about the reform that had just taken place at the Comédie Française—everyone, that is, except the object of the reform, the *petits marquis* who had just been banished from the stage. The *petits marquis* reacted with anger. Much less concerned about the future of French theatre than about their own present, the *petits marquis* resorted to mayhem across the street at the Café Procope. As described by Bonnassies, "The *petits-maîtres* were infuriated; that very evening there was a terrible outburst at the Procope: swords were drawn, and the chandeliers and mirrors of the café paid for the carrying off of the *secchia.*"[12]

As a 1762 account suggests, the social style of this constituency was indeed cramped by the reform.

> One doesn't see them anymore at the theatre, flitting from box to box, playing monkey through the hole in the curtain, insolently ogling the most honest women, smiling at them without knowing them; crossing the stage twenty times, harrassing the actresses in the green-rooms, watching them take off their costumes, and escorting them afterwards, dressed as nymphs, for a snack outside the city gates.[13]

The alternatives thereafter available to the displaced *petit-maîtres* are facetiously outlined in a 1765 play performed at the Comédie Italienne. A *marquis,* sophisticated in the ways of Paris, gives advice to a country baron:

> Should you wish to appear somebody in society:
> . . . .
> Arrive at the day's play with great brio,

Enter each box, though you have nothing to say,
Stay only time enough to show your outfit,
In the middle of the green-rooms, collect an uproarious crowd,
On the staircase, confide secrets aloud.
In an impatient tone, call your valets,
etc.[14]

The *petits marquis* may have attempted to carry on as before, but their antics were confined to private boxes, the greenrooms and the staircase—places that were all quite harmless to the spectacle on the stage.

The Comédie Italienne

In the meantime, the Comédie Italienne, which in reality had become a second French troupe and fierce competitor of the Comédie Française, still played in a theatre which, despite some hasty refurbishing in 1716 and 1742, had remained virtually unmodified since the middle of the seventeenth century.[15] Nothing had as yet been done to cope with the *petit marquis* problem at the Hôtel de Bourgogne, perhaps because stage decoration, for one reason or another, had not been as neglected at the Comédie Italienne as it had been at the Comédie Française. According to Blondel in 1754, "the reproach of [lack of stage decoration] cannot be made to the Comédiens Italiens, who in truth probably need this accessory to attract the curiosity of the spectators."[16] In 1760, however, the Italian troupe undertook extensive remodeling which, among other things, provided for clearance of spectators from the stage.[17] Faced with a much larger project than the French troupe, the Comédie Italienne found it necessary to move out of the Hôtel de Bourgogne for a period of five months. During the summer and autumn of 1760, from May 10 to October 8, the troupe occupied the so-called Salle des Ramparts, located on one of the boulevards laid out along the city's old ramparts.[18]

During the troupe's absence from the Hôtel de Bourgogne, the area formerly given over to the *petits-maîtres* was thoroughly restructured. The tiered benches were removed from either side of the stage, to be partially replaced by double Corinthian columns which formed the base of the new proscenium arch. The *Spectacles de Paris* described the transformations:

> The benches on the forestage have been done away with, replaced, on each side of the stage, by two coupled Corinthian columns with channeled molding, painted in white veined marble, with gilded bases and capitols. They are in half-round, set on a simple pedestal, and surmounted by an architrave cornice, also gilded, which continues in a straight line from one side of the stage to the other. The soffit is painted with charming ornaments, highlighted with gold; all of that makes up the forestage.[19]

The three tiers of existing stage boxes *(balcons)* were left in place behind the proscenium arch, but were freshly and elaborately decorated. Again the

Spectacles de Paris: "Near these columns are the stage boxes, which have been
kept, but whose fronts are now joined together and flush; the second and third
tiers are painted to resemble a mosaic, with open-work trim and gilded
checkerboard edging." According to the *Mercure de France,* the stage boxes
were "very beautifully composed," and much admired by artists.[20] And, like at
the Comédie Française, screened boxes *(loges grillées)* providing great privacy
were constructed underneath the remaining stage boxes, at eye-level with the
stage floor. "Below is a secret box, whose wrought iron open-work grill is at
stage level; this grill is gilded," reported the *Mercure.* Two new staircases were
constructed "within the depths of the forestage . . . leading to all the stage boxes
and to the screened boxes located under the stage." Figure 37, showing the
Hôtel de Bourgogne ca. 1772 after still further remodeling, offers a detailed
illustration of some of these changes.[21]

In addition to the changes on the forestage, more choice seating was
provided in the *parterre* area. Still according to the *Mercure,* "a *parquet* was
formed, behind the orchestra, which encroached on the *parterre.*" This new
parquet contained seven enormous benches running across the width of the
salle. As compared to benches known to seat 4, these new benches could
probably accommodate as many as 20 persons each, such that at least 140
spectators could be seated in the *parquet*[22] (see figs. 37 and 38).

No information has yet come to light indicating what the seating capacity
of the stage benches at the Comédie Italienne had been in 1760. Thornhill's
1717 sketch indicates only two rows of benches on either side of the stage,
which, given the weak attendance at the Comédie Italienne, may or may not
have been subsequently augmented. We therefore cannot gauge to what extent
the new seating arrangement compensated, or perhaps even overcompensated,
for the loss of stage seating.

It is clear, however, that after remodeling, the Comédie Italienne, like the
Comédie Française, had a stage opening of some thirty feet at the front (four
toises, one *pied,* or 8.12 meters, as calculated by Lagrave), and could undertake
the same kind of productions as its rival. According to the *Année littéraire:*
"The stage is very spacious and fit for the performance of spectacle plays.
Eliminated from the framework have been a *patte d'oie* and a *croupe,* all the
more bothersome in that no machines could be brought into play. The great
height prevailing at present will facilitate their use."[23] It was these same
structural changes which, of course, paved the way for the Comédie Italienne to
become the Opéra Comique in 1762.

The remodeling, together with a new curtain and much gilt and
ornamentation throughout the *salle,* were well received. According to a
contemporary observer, "the public, though it misses the old forestage . . .
seemed very satisfied with the new arrangement, which spoiled nothing in that
theatre."[24] And, to be sure, the changes seem to have infused new life into the

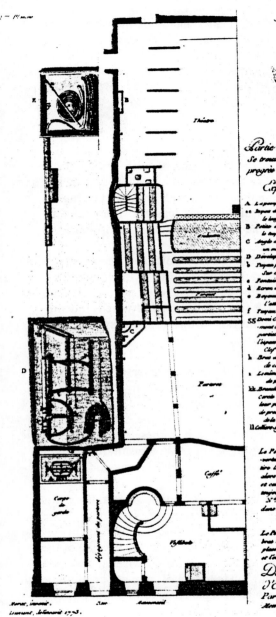

Figure 38.   Partial Plan, Comédie Italienne
Hôtel de Bourgogne, 1773
(Dumont, *Parallèle des plans*)

ailing Comédie Italienne. The *registre* for the October 8 reopening of the Hôtel de Bourgogne shows a sudden surge of ticket sales, including many rentals of entire boxes to theatre-goers eager to have a look at the sparkling new house and its stage devoid of *petits-maîtres*. It is interesting to note that the lower stage boxes, that is, those just above where the stage benches had been, remained a male preserve. The well-fed, well-dressed torsos of their distinguished occupants can be made out in figure 37.

Spectators on the Stage after the Reform

The official interdiction of spectators on the stages of both the Comédie Française and the Comédie Italienne did not mean the de facto end of this practice. On the contrary, at both those theatres, as well as at the Opéra, on-stage seating was routinely offered on certain special occasions. These were the so-called "capitation" performances at the Opéra, and gratis performances at the other two theatres.

Capitation performances were essentially benefit nights for members of the Opéra troupe. All money taken in on these occasions was distributed on a pro rata basis to troupe members.[25] Authorized by royal ordinance, capitation performances took place as many as six times per year, and were frequently followed by a ball.[26] Clearly, the best interests of the troupe were served by packing as many spectators as possible into the theatre for such events. Though standard royal ordinances forbade the presence of spectators on the stage of the Opéra under normal circumstances, their presence was expressly permitted at capitation performances, "His Majesty...permitting them in this case...to distribute, for these performances only, stage tickets."[27] And, indeed, those nostalgic over lost privilege were apparently attracted to these gala affairs in large numbers. The price of admittance to the stage at these events was one louis, and on at least one occasion "the number of these pleasant individuals was so large that the *parterre* took offense, made a devilish row and obliged them to withdraw to the wings."[28]

Those with a taste for such activity could also sit on the stage at the gratis performances periodically offered to the public at large. To be sure, free performances attracted a very different crowd from that in attendance at capitation events. The custom at gratis performances was to reserve all of the stage boxes *(balcons)* on the queen's side of the house for fishwives and women merchants of Les Halles, and on the king's side, opposite, to place an all-male contingent of coal merchants. But despite this plebeian element, it was still customary for seats on the stage itself to be occupied by aristocracy, who "paid" for their seats by distributing gold louis to less fortunate attendees. The *Mercure* reports, relative to a gratis performance of the new and highly successful *Siège de Calais* by de Belloy on March 12, 1765, that "there were about fifty louis distributed at that performance, by M. le Maréchal de Biron ... as well as by several lords and ladies placed on the stage, and by each actor and actress."[29]

At least once, in 1778, it was the *poissardes* and *charbonniers* themselves who occupied the stage benches, an enormous turnout for *Zaïre* having upset the usual order of things.

> Whatever precautions were taken to save the King's box for the coal-merchants, where they are accustomed to sitting on such occasions (in the same way that the fishwives sit in the Queen's box), their places were all taken by the time they arrived. They were offered admittance to the stage, and they seated themselves there, still on the King's side, on some benches that had been prepared. The fishwives, not wanting to lose sight of them, asked to leave the Queen's box, and went up on the stage where they formed a row parallel to that of the coal-merchants.[30]

Apart from gratis and capitation performances, spectators appeared on stage from time to time in entirely unscheduled fashion. Upon the debut in 1772 of Mlle Raucourt at the Comédie Française (recently installed at the Tuileries theatre), "the crowd was such that it was necessary to let it overflow into the orchestra pit and even onto the stage."[31] A similar incident occurred at the Comédie Italienne (by then officially known as the Opéra Comique) in 1784.

> The closing performance at the Comédie Italienne was remarkable only for the great tumult occasioned by the sight of a prodigious crowd on the stage when the curtain went up. The players being unable to begin, the curtain was lowered, and an attempt was made to move back the spectators who were offending the public. This arrangement did not satisfy those who were annoyed: the hue and cry did not cease, soldiers were brought to the *parterre;* such a measure caused even more irritation; an arrest of someone was attempted; everyone defended him; it was declared that they would not tolerate his being led away; they scuffled with the guard; then an officer came and ordered the soldiers to withdraw. Mr. Thomassin [a celebrated actor] decided to address the public, to offer apologies on behalf of the troupe, to beg that an exception be granted this one time; he appealed for the indulgence of the assembly; ... the noise came to an end.[32]

The seating of spectators on the stage probably continued to be standard practice in small commercial theatres well beyond its discontinuation in the official theatres. Spectators behind a balustrade can be seen, for instance, in two illustrations depicting performances by one of the numerous children's troupes (such as Les Petits Comédiens du Roi, Les Petits Comédiens du Bois de Boulogne) which sprang up in the second half of the century[33] (see figs. 12 and 13).

The persistence of certain old habits notwithstanding, change was clearly in the air. The year 1759, in addition to reform on the stage of the Comédie Française, had also seen establishment of the first *théâtre du boulevard*, the Nicolet Theatre. In 1762, two years after spectators were removed from the stage of the Comédie Italienne, the Comédie Italienne became known as the Opéra Comique and was largely given over to musical productions. At the Comédie Française, in the meantime, a new era had begun. The new visual dimension rendered possible by a cleared stage, taken together with the new emotional dimension of the *drame,* was to carry French theatre rapidly away from the rigors and constraints of classicism. The next chapter will discuss some of the ways in which the evolving visual aesthetic was expressed on a stage freed of spectators.

Spectators on the Stage in Other Countries

The *Année littéraire,* in 1758, had deplored the "ridiculous habit" which, it claimed, was "established only in France."[34] The claim was, of course, erroneous, for France was not alone in having to cope with the problem of spectators on the stage. The practice of viewing a play from the stage became fashionable in England earlier, and, despite many attempts at reform, lasted longer, than in France. Shortly after the beginning of the seventeenth century, young gallants began seating themselves on the stage on small three-legged stools provided by the actors for an extra fee. The practice was well enough established by 1609 that Thomas Dekker's "Gull's Hornbook" gives advice about it. In a chapter called "How a gallant is to behave himself in a theatre," the guidebook counsels: "present not your selfe on the stage (especially at a new play) until the ... prologue is ready to enter;" for if an entrance is made "when the belly of the house is but half full, your apparel is quite eaten up, the fashion lost." When, after the twenty-year closure which commenced in 1642, theatre life once again resumed, the dandies took up where they had left off. In 1665 an order pertaining to one of the London theatres forbade any but actors "to enter at the door of the Attiring-house" (the stage door leading to the dressing rooms).[35]

Spectators on the English stage were still a problem in the first part of the eighteenth century. A proclamation issued by Queen Anne on January 17, 1704 stipulated "that no person of what quality soever presume to go behind the scenes or come upon the stage, either before or during the the acting of a play."[36] Colley Cibber's dedication to his *Lady's Last Stake* (1708), Steele's *Spectator* Numbers 220 and 224 (1711), the *Weekly Journal* in 1718 and James Ralph's *The Touch-Stone* (1728), all give accounts of the continuing nuisance created by the young gentlemen who insisted upon admittance to the stage.

The custom evolved differently in England than in France. In France, the presence of spectators on the stage, though railed against and decried, was technically accepted. Permanent accommodation—benches, a solidly fixed balustrade, carpeting—were provided, while ordinances and proclamations were designed not to forbid the entrance of Parisian dandies to the stage altogether, but to control their behavior once they were there. In England, on the other hand, theatres did not provide permanent seating for stage spectators: the strategy was to attempt to discourage spectators from reaching the stage in the first place. However, at benefit performances (much more prevalent in England than in France) special provisions were made in the form of temporary amphitheatres built on the stage. Super-crowded and festive, these performances elicited a tolerant atmosphere that seemed to bring out the most eccentric in stage spectator behavior. Those concerned with the welfare of English theatre were never in doubt that spectators on the stage ultimately had to be banished.

Many efforts were made to prevent spectators from going "behind the scenes" and onto the stage, but neither official proclamations nor periodic campaigns by theatre managers proved effective. Colley Cibber, writing in 1740, boasts of having removed spectators from the stage of the Drury Lane some years earlier.

> Among our many necessary Reformations what not a little preserv'd to us the Regard of our Auditors, was the Decency of our clear Stage; from whence we had now, for many Years, shut out those idle Gentlemen....[37]

Yet the problem persisted, at the frequent benefit performances, if not at the others. At the start of the 1740-41 season, Covent Garden bills announced that their "entertainment" of *Orpheus and Eurydice*, depending for its effect largely on its scenic devices, required an absolutely clear stage, and that gentlemen must therefore be "refused Admission behind the Scenes." During the next season Drury Lane followed suit.[38] However, the young dandies continued to frequent the stage. When Garrick assumed the management of Drury Lane in 1747, he made an immediate attempt at reform. The opening night playbill announcing *The Merchant of Venice* carried a notice that no money was to be taken "for the future" for admission behind the scenes. But that effort was no more successful than the others.

Lasting reform was not to come until fifteen years later, in 1762, when, perhaps following the example from across the Channel, Garrick enlarged the auditorium in such a way that the actors' benefit income would not be reduced.

The practice of seating spectators on the stage was exported to Germany in at least one instance. Goethe, recollecting his attendance at the Frankfort theatre as a young boy in 1759, describes what he saw when, in the wake of the French occupation of Frankfort during the Seven Years War, a French theatre troupe took up residence in a converted concert hall.

[The proscenium] was very deep, after the French style, and was bordered on both sides with seats, which, surrounded by a low rail, ascended in several rows one behind another, so that the first seats were but a little elevated above the stage. The whole was considered a place of special honour, and was generally used only by officers. . . . If, when the house was very full at such time as troops were passing through the town, officers of distinction strove for this place of honour, which was generally occupied already, some rows of benches and chairs were placed in the proscenium on the stage itself, and nothing remained for the heroes and heroines but to reveal their secrets in the very limited space between the uniforms and orders.[39]

The custom of admitting gentlemen to the stage seems not to have taken hold at all in either Spain or Italy. An exception in Spain was the occasional presence of a Royal Magistrate. Writing in 1738, Riccoboni reports that, during plays for which the stage decoration was simple rather than elaborate, the *Alcade de Corte* "occupies a chair on one side of the Stage, with two or three Archers from his entourage placed behind him."[40] The fact that Italy remained free of spectators on the stage is confirmed in some letters from an eighteenth-century French visitor to Italy. Writing from Genoa in 1739, Charles de Brosses, a public figure and distinguished man of letters, reports that "here men do not take seats on the stage . . . but on a platform at stage level, situated just below the boxes and above and around the *parterre:* upon rising from their benches at intermission, they are within conversational range of the women who are in the boxes."[41] Later, in a letter from Rome, he writes: "Spectators never sit on the stage, not at the theatre nor at the opera; only in France do we have this ridiculous habit of occupying a space meant only for actors and scenery."[42] De Brosses, of course, was wrong, for the "ridiculous habit" was still very much a plague in the English theatre and remained so for a time to come.

8

Effect on Stage Decoration

Available space on the stage of the Comédie Française was, as we have seen, rendered essentially double by the departure of the *petits marquis*. Moreover, virtually all of the wing flats and wing openings were now usable as intended, for entrances and exits, and most of all, for stage decoration and lighting. Unlike what is sometimes believed, stage decoration during the period preceding the removal of spectators from the stage had not been entirely absent. However, the possibilities for elaborate décor and imposing crowd scenes once stage seating ended must have seemed limitless after decades of contending with a stage that was sometimes little more than an aisle between two hedgerows of overdressed dandies. Starved for the long-absent visual element, playwrights and stage decorators rushed to fill the void, and a new order of spectacular stage effect was quickly achieved.

Stage Decoration before 1759

It has been often assumed that there was almost no stage decoration during the last half of the seventeenth century and the first half of the eighteenth, and that the presence of spectators on the stage was directly responsible for this state of affairs. Modern scholarship has shown, however, that this assessment is simplistic. "We cannot believe, as Rigal does," writes T.E. Lawrenson in 1957, "that the 'scène simultanée' was condemned in 1636 by the first appearance of the seigneurs on either side of the forestage, much less that after that date 'there was hardly more than a backdrop for stage decoration' for all the evidence of the *Mémoire* [*de Mahelot*] is against this."[1] The simplification of stage decoration which occurred during the preclassical period in France was, rather, an outgrowth of a developing taste for the unities which antedated the regular appearance of spectators on the stage. The time was ripe: authors, actors and public were tiring of baroque complexities, and were ready for a change of approach in the theatre. It might even be argued that had stage decoration not already not been in the process of evolving towards simplicity, the practice of seating play-goers on the stage might not have flourished as it did.[2]

Even before Jean de Mairet's *Sophonisbe* in 1634, there was movement towards espousal of the restrictive rules of classical antiquity. In 1630 and 1631—several years before the first evidence of nobility on the stage—authors were already attempting to apply the unity of time in their works: Gombaud in *L'Amaranthe* (1630); Pichou in *Filis de Scire* (1630); Claveret in *L'Esprit fort* (1630); Corneille in *Clitandre* (1631); Boisrobert in *L'Heureuse tromperie* (1631); Rotrou in *Ménechmes* (1630 or 1631). This interest in the unities led, before long, to simplification of stage decoration, most notably to a reduction in the number of compartments or *mansions* on the stage. Spearheading this movement was Jean de Mairet's *Sophonisbe* (1634), which called for two adjoining rooms in a palace, separated by a tapestry, and for a public square in front of the palace. The usual five compartments indicated by Mahelot were thus reduced to two or three. Other early plays with simplified stage decoration were Corneille's *Place Royale* (1634) and *Le Menteur* (1642) and Scudéry's *L'Amant libéral* (1636-37).

The first production of the *Cid* made use of the traditional five compartments, but subsequently, and no doubt for reasons responsive to the presence of Chevaliers de l'Ordre on stage, this style of decor was abandoned in favor of a setting depicting a single place.[3] Tristan l'Hermite's *La Mort de Crispe* presented by the Illustre Théâtre in 1644 had a single setting representing an interior. *Cinna* (1642) calls for two rooms in a palace, though in performance only a single room was actually displayed.[4] *Horace* (1640), *Polyeucte* (1641-42) and *La Mort de Pompée* (1642) call for a single room only. Corneille makes a point of saying that "unity of place occurs" in *Rodogugne* (1644). Authors spoke of their espousal of the unities with pride, not irritation. The change was voluntary rather than imposed by external circumstance: Mahelot's system of simultaneous decor had simply gone out of style, replaced by the *palais à volonté* and its variants. The *palais à volonté* (loosely translatable as "whatever kind of palace you please"), was often a courtyard-like setting with columns and an opening at the back revealing a vista of seascape, landscape, battle encampment, or the like. These imposing yet indeterminate settings were architecturally suitable for tragedy and permitted the playing of diverse scenes without danger of breaking the new rules. The simplicity and dignity of the *palais à volonté* must have been perceived as a welcome antidote to the confusion of five compartments, sometimes with painted curtains in front to create additional locations.[5] The new simplified stage decoration was thus the result not of a revolution, but of an evolution which had been taking place from the early 1630s on, under the ever-increasing influence of *les règles dramatiques* (the rules) adapted from classical antiquity and transmitted, via Scaliger, Vida and Castelvetro, by the doctrine of Chapelain and others in France.

The theatre troupes, too, contributed to this evolution, if perhaps only for somewhat ulterior motives at first. What historians of the theatre now view as desirable simplification of stage decoration was then sometimes seen as stringency and impoverishment, a state of affairs sometimes blamed on the miserliness of theatre troupes. Their members accepted the stripping down of stage settings called for by the precepts of classicism without much objection, since only minimal expenditures were necessary to build the simplified sets. The theatre-going public, too, played its part in this evolution. More refined and sophisticated in the second half of the century than in the first, audiences seemed to accept and even welcome the lack of spectacular stage decoration.

The fact that stage decoration was evolving in the direction of minimalism from the 1630s on does not mean, as is sometimes mistakenly believed, that there was virtually no decoration at all other than the *toile de fond* (backdrop). Machine plays, of course, were notorious for their expensive and elaborate settings, but straight dramatic fare also made substantial use of stage decoration. At times stage decoration was more elaborate than at other times, but there was always some kind of décor. As Jacques Vanuxem has explained, "The idea of performing on a bare stage never occurred to anybody in the seventeenth century; however miserable, the performance was surrounded with tapestries and painted scene-drops, and the actors made an effort, sometimes with scant resources, to evoke a certain display of costumes. At the court or in Paris, decor was very rich, as were the costumes."[6] Indeed, there are many references in dramatic texts to stage decoration. Characters in tragedies speak of "the splendor of this place," "this magnificent palace," "these splendid monuments," texts which would be nonsense if stage decoration did not exist.

It was equally true, however, that the presence of spectators on the stage acted as a limiting factor to stage decorations. Elaborate changes of scenery, not wanted anyway in straight dramatic fare, were also not possible. While backdrops might be changed as desired, decoration nearer the front of the stage was less flexible. In any case, public taste for the visually spectacular was satisfied not by the growing repertory of neoclassical tragedies and comedies, but by the burgeoning of *pièces à machines,* and by the development of *grand spectacle* at the Opéra. Stage settings for this type of production were becoming more and more complicated at the same time that, for other genres, décor was growing simpler.

If the presence of forty or fifty spectators on the stage during the second half of the seventeenth century did not prevent or even seriously inhibit whatever stage decoration was desired at that juncture, that was not the case at all after the turn of the century. Once again, tastes were changing: the pendulum was swinging back from whence it had come. Just as a reaction to theatrical austerity was beginning to set in, certain material changes having to do with the seating of spectators on the stage created significant interference with the development of décor. The installation in 1689 of a wrought iron balustrade on either side of the stage of the Comédie Française acted as a permanent barrier to any kind of activity involving the first and second wing openings. An even more serious blow was dealt by the sharp increase early in the eighteenth century in the number of benches on the stage, from four rows (two on either side of the stage) to a total of ten. As we have seen in an earlier chapter, the area defined by the balustrades thus took up nearly half of the stage area, leaving an aperture of only fifteen *pieds* at stage front, and eleven at the rear. The curtailment of available acting surface was drastic.

Changes of stage setting could readily be effected by manipulation of the wing flats during the intermission between the tragedy and the comedy being presented on a given day, but changes during the course of a play were largely confined to the raising and lowering of backdrops. Gently chiding the Comédie Française, the architect Blondel describes the facilities at that theatre (the description can be followed visually in fig. 9):

> The mobile decorations for this stage begin only after the pilasters labeled X, called *Proscenium*, and consist of six wings on each side, labeled Y, which are only changed if, following performance of a tragedy, there is to be an intermission, and a comedy requiring a special decor. The flats Z, most of which are only curtains that are raised or lowered, are sometimes used during the course of a play to effect various changes in the different scenes of a tragedy or comedy.... [T]his theatre, greatly esteemed as it is, would seem to require particular attention to decoration on the part of the troupe, in order to live up to the expectations of the public and to the esteem in which it is held by thoughtful men and connoisseurs.[7]

Another important visual element affected by the physical constraints of so many spectators on the stage was, of course, the ability of actors and actresses to move around. When the stage was packed with 230 spectators or more, the players could do little more than engage in animated conversation near the front of the stage, directing their speeches to the audience standing in the *parterre*. The plays of Corneille and Racine, in their classical purity, may not have suffered severely from such treatment. But Voltaire's plays, and those of others attempting to develop the use of pantomime and other visual techniques, were another matter.

The simple lack of space on the stage was not the only way in which the presence of spectators on the stage affected stage decoration and visual impact. The problem of lighting was an additional factor.[8] The two large chandeliers which hung above either side of the stage of the Comédie Française, and which were lighted before the spectacle began, could be raised and lowered at any time. They could not, however, be extinguished during the performance because of their position over the heads of the *petits marquis* (see fig. 39). Thus,

Figure 39.   Lowered Theatre Curtain
Coypel, 1726
(Bibliothèque Nationale, Cabinet des Estampes)

the stage could never be totally darkened during a performance, nor could much subtlety of lighting be achieved. In his *Lettre sur les Spectacles* Crébillon wrote that the chandeliers

> often gave the lie to certain decorations. How to convince oneself, for example, that one was in a garden, or out in the countryside, or in Agamemnon's camp, when the candles hanging from the ceiling assaulted the eyes and the noses of the spectators?[9]

The ruinous distraction resulting from the fact that the spectators on the stage were as well-lighted as the actors on the stage has been discussed in an earlier section.

The possibility of stage spectators interfering with the stage curtain also worked against visual effect. Spectators sitting on the stage not only might find themselves in the path of the descending curtain, but might also sometimes actively impede its trajectory. Sabbattini, writing in Italy in 1638, hence not addressing himself directly to the French problem of spectators on the stage, but rather to the problem of spectators versus the curtain in general, advised that:

> A little before the curtain is raised, some faithful persons should be placed in front at the parapet to prevent anyone from coming near the curtain, thus avoiding dangers and confusions, such as sometimes occur because of malice, negligence or lack of discretion of the stage hands who hold the ends of the curtain.[10]

This problem, surely accentuated by the onset of stage seating, may have come under somewhat better control after balustrades were installed. However, if Coypel's 1726 depiction of the stage curtain at the Comédie Française is any indication (fig. 39), the problem was far from eliminated.

New Visual Effects

Despite the fact that it was difficult to effect changes of scenery in the eighteenth century, and that there was almost no room for stage properties, playwrights still attempted to create visual interest. Caught up in the evolving esthetic of the *drame* and related genres, authors kept trying to create plays that were imagined as if all of the above material constraints did not exist. The mood in theatre as the century progressed and as authors experimented outside the purist precepts of classicism, was in the direction of greater visual effect.

Prior to removal of spectators from the stage, appeal to the eye at the Comédie Française, apart, of course, from that formerly offered by machine plays,[11] had been limited. For the 1742-43 season, new opera-style decorations making use of the full height of the stage were designed by Roberto Clerici de Parme, a pupil of the Bibiena brothers, for revivals of Racine's *Athalie* and La

Grange-Chancel's *Ino et Mélicerte,* as well as for Voltaire's *Oedipe.*[12] In 1755, Chateaubrun's *Philoctète* presented a view of a cave, and Voltaire's *Orphelin de la Chine,* a Chinese palace as well as Chinese and Tartar costumes. *Sémiramis* (1748) and *Oreste* (1750), the most spectacular plays given while a portion of the audience crowded the stage, showed a palace, a temple, a tomb and other sights of interest.[13] In *Sémiramis,* for instance, when the curtain opened, the stage was supposed to represent "a vast peristyle at the end of which is the palace of Sémiramis. Terrassed gardens rise above the palace. The temple of the priests is to the right, and a mausoleum to the left, decorated with obelisks."[14] Succeeding acts represented scenes inside the palace, in the vestibule of a temple and outside a mausoleum. Although the text of the play calls for four different settings, the solution actually adopted by the decorators (the Slodtz brothers) was very much akin to the long-forgotten simultaneous decor of the baroque era.[15] Valiant efforts were clearly being made to decorate the stage, despite all obstacles.

After 1759, however, stage decorators were able to practice their craft in vastly improved conditions. Although the existence of stage boxes still precluded decoration of the forestage, the wings had been liberated, and were usable as intended for the first time ever at the Ancienne Comédie. Moreover, without the presence of spectators on the stage, audiences could see settings in their entirety, and perceive a given stage decoration as a coherent picture. Authors and decorators hastened to fill the empty stage and its six restored wing openings with a variety of visual delights. Once again, Voltaire led the way. *Sémiramis,* the play which a decade earlier had been undermined by the presence of *petits marquis,* was performed for the first time on the newly cleared stage in August of 1759. The decorator Brunetti designed a new and grandiose set showing Semiramis' palace against a panorama of the Euphrates and the town of Babylon.[16] Lekain provided 45 supernumeraries: "a palace lady, 8 satraps, 2 chiefs and 12 soldiers, 20 men of the people, 2 officers."[17] The improvement was duly noted by the *Mercure.*

> The tragedy of *Sémiramis* has been brought back to the stage. Never have all the advantages of the changes made to the stage appeared more brilliant; nor ever have the great tableaux of this very theatrical and moving tragedy so deeply affected the audience. Although the forestage decorations are not sufficiently in harmony with the back of the stage, the general impression remains imposing.[18]

And, unlike the 1748 production of Voltaire's play, this one made use of *successive* rather than simultaneous settings, just as at the Opéra.[19]

The décor of Racine's *Iphigénie* was also dramatically improved soon after departure of the *petits-maîtres* from the stage. The opening scene of this tragedy is meant to show Agamemnon awakening in his tent while night still reigns in the camp. Prior to reform, a standard set called "Le camp" was used for this play (Mahelot specifies that the "stage is tents and, in the back, a sea and some vessels"), and only Agamemnon's tent was represented separately. An already-lighted chandelier cast its light from above upon the ruler's tent. Afterwards, however, this opening scene was greatly altered. Brunetti was commissioned to paint five large set pieces representing not only Agamemnon's tent, but Achille's as well. When the curtain rose the audience beheld a Greek camp in total darkness, save for Agamemnon's tent which was was now illuminated from the inside only. A long, purely pantomime sequence then showed Agamemnon sealing an envelope, leaving his tent to look for Archas, while around him day was slowly breaking and sleeping soldiers were awakening and taking up their posts. The dramatic impact of this new opening scene for *Iphigénie* was much appreciated by the public. "All that is within the realm of exact truth," wrote one commentator, "and contributes to the theatrical illusion."[20]

Lekain took charge of creating new productions for other plays already in the repertory at the Comédie Française, and thanks to the careful notes he kept, left a record of the changes that were made.[21] The first thing Lekain did was abandon for once and for all the *palais à volonté* that had been standard for classical tragedy from Mahelot's time onward. Lekain's aim was to give each play its own décor, meant to be suited to its subject. For *Andromaque*, it was "a Greek-style gallery adjacent to several rooms." The *Cid* took place not in "a room with four doors," but in the three different settings called for by the text: "Chimène's appartment, adorned with the gothic architecture in use in the eleventh century;" the king's palace and "a public square in complete darkness."[22]

New sets were also provided for certain plays in which changes of scene had always been symbolically indicated by the carrying on or off of a particular stage property. In Voltaire's *Brutus*, for instance, the stage directions specify that "The temple of the Capitol can be seen in the background. The senators are assembled between the temple and the house; before the altar of Mars . . . the senators are positioned in a semicircle."[23] In practice, the altar of Mars was brought on stage to suggest the public square in front of the temple of the Capitol, and was removed again when the scene changed to the consular house.[24] In *Mérope*, the *valets de théâtre* would carry in a tomb to signify that the action had moved to a churchyard. Now Brunetti executed special scenery for such scenes, creating entire sets for the Roman public square in *Brutus* and the churchyard in *Mérope*.[25]

As for the creation of new works, Voltaire was once more in the forefront. Despite a coquettish declaration that Rousseau's "Lettre sur les spectacles" was causing him to renounce the theatre,[26] the prospect of an unencumbered stage immediately stimulated Voltaire to create *Tancrède*. "Mon cher ange," he exulted to d'Argental in mid-May of 1759, "I told you that liberty and honor

restored to the French stage would rouse my old brain;" and, in the dedication
to Mme de Pompadour: "I outlined [the play] the minute I knew that the Paris
stage was changed, and was becoming a real theatre." His express intention in
Tancrède was to take advantage of the newly available stage space to appeal to
the eye. "Mon Dieu! how pleased I was when I learned that the stage was
purged of white-faces, coifed like a rhinoceros or a royal bird! I was laughing to
the skies while filling in the scene with the shields and the banners," he wrote
d'Argental, and, in the dedication: "You have to strike the soul and the eye at
once."[27] To this end, Brunetti created a spectacular décor. In addition to the
display of chivalric paraphernalia, shields, lances and six enormous banners
suspended over the public square,[28] *Tancrède* offered spectacular crowd
scenes. At the first performance (September 3, 1760), sixty-six supernumeraries were employed, costumed as medieval knights, their followers, or
citizens of Syracuse. Taking full advantage of an acting surface which had
doubled in size, *Tancrède* was exemplary in its use of large groups of actors.[29]

Following the lead of *Tancrède,* other playwrights came forth with works
calling for spectacular productions. In 1760, Colardeau's *Caliste* featured
funereal hangings, the stage directions indicating that "The stage is draped in
black, and is only faintly lit; a lamp is suspended in the middle."[30] The
following year, plays such as Lemierre's *Terrée* and Diderot's *Père de famille*
made use of the cleared stage to present carefully constructed tableaux.
Diderot's lengthy stage directions specify that

> The stage represents a parlor, decorated with tapestries, mirrors, pictures, a clock,
> etc.... Towards the front of the room, the father of the family paces slowly.... Towards the
> back, near the fireplace which is on one side of the room, the Commander and his niece are
> playing backgammon. Behind the Commander, a little closer to the fire, Germeuil is lounging
> in the armchair, a book in hand.

In 1762, de Belloy's *Zelmire* filled the stage with soldiers and priests moving
against a landscape of trees, rocks, a road, a temple and a tomb surrounded by
cypress trees. In 1764 Voltaire's *Olympie* outdid *Tancrède* as a spectacle with
eighty-three supernumeraries and a funeral pyre. A funeral pyre was also seen
in Lemierre's *La Veuve du Malabar* (1770), while his *Guillaume Tell* (1765)
offered a wild and mountainous setting representing "the area around a lake
where craggy rocks can be seen piled up to the clouds."[31] Attributed to
Brunetti, and the object of much comment, this striking set broke the
perspective of the wings, and featured twenty-five foot high trees in the
foreground.[32] Sauvigny's *Hirza ou l'Illinois* (1767) presented no less a spectacle
than Niagara Falls and a tomb decorated by Indians.

> In the background can be seen Niagara Falls. To one side, craggy rocks, some cabins and
> some trees; on the other, a tomb standing on *matachés* pillars, and decorated with hair in the
> form of a trophy; at the foot of the tomb is an altar on which have been placed the weapons of
> the defunct, his arrows, his tomahawk and his manitou.[33]

A comparison of these plays with those written shortly before by some of the same authors can leave no doubt as to how eager playwrights were to make use of the crowd scenes and abundant scenery that had now become feasible at the Comédie Française.

Even more spectacular effects became possible upon transfer of the Comédie Française to the cavernous Tuileries Theatre in 1770.[34] The use of crowd scenes doubtless reached its outer limit when, for the first production of *Régulus* in 1773, Dorat employed no fewer than 320 supernumeraries![35] The stage was decorated in equally grandiose fashion. Not content to paint the largest backdrop he had ever done (a panoramic view of Rome), Brunetti also built a sailing ship that was more than twenty-three *pieds* long and twenty high.[36]

Two versions of *Oedipe*, one written early in the century and the other much later, also offer a measure of the progress that was made. Voltaire's *Oedipe* (1718) specifies only that at play's end "Lightning flashes and thunder can be heard." But by the time Ducis composed his *Oedipe chez Admète* in 1778, a more elaborate effect was possible.

> The door to the inside of the temple opens, incense is smoking, the figures of the Eumenides can be seen, the instruments necessary for sacrifices, and in general everything that can characterize the temple of the Furies: an altar is in the center: the flame is shining . . . lightning flashes, a thunderbolt rumbles, explodes, and overturns Oedipus.[37]

On a stage that could be decorated as far forward as desired, settings of greater depth could be imagined. While simple thunder and lightning had had to serve as climax to Voltaire's play, sixty years later, Ducis was able to portray in addition the mystery and drama of a glimpse of the inner sanctum of the temple of the Furies.

A stage cleared of spectators also allowed improvements in lighting. To be sure, great progress in this direction had already taken place before 1759. In the early part of the eighteenth century, most of the light which fell on the stage came from a number of chandeliers suspended above it. As reported by the *Mercure Galant*, the Comédie Française in 1689 had twenty-four such chandeliers. "The auditorium appeared that day in full beauty, lighted by 24 chandeliers bearing candles, whose light brought out the paintings and made the ornaments shine."[38] Records indicate that by 1719 the stage of the Comédie Française was ordinarily illuminated from above by 120 tallow candles *(chandelles)* most likely arrayed in ten chandeliers *(lustres)* with 12 candles each. The *rampe*, or footlights, consisted of forty-eight candles the same size as those in the chandeliers, and there were forty-eight additional candles of somewhat smaller size distributed among the wings. However as optical research progressed in the middle eighteenth century, stage lighting improved and became more subtle. Chandelier lighting was reduced, while footlight and wing lighting was intensified.[39]

In 1759, the footlights consisted of thirty-two large oil lamps or *bisquits* which could be raised and lowered. Now the stage was lighted by means of a *rampe* (footlights) and *portants* (wing-ladders). The footlights were placed on a kind of a retractable trap door thirty centimeters wide. Two of these devices ran along the front edge of the stage, each one covering half of the stage, starting at the side of the stage and running towards the center as far as the prompter's box. For a darkened stage, the trap doors were retracted below stage level and the light from the wing-ladders or *portants* was masked by a shutter. For scenes meant to take place indoors at night, a chandelier was lowered from the flies above the stage. There were now over one hundred candles in the wings, where in 1719 there had been only forty-eight. Because lighting after the abolition of stage seating could be established in natural-seeming places on the stage itself (candles on tables, mantelpieces), as well as from the newly liberated wings, it became possible to reduce considerably the number of obtrusive chandeliers hanging from above. "The lighting has been redistributed in such a way that no more than four chandeliers with candles are visible," comments the *Année littéraire*.[40] Though the number of chandeliers had been reduced, the total candlepower which illuminated the stage was greater. Lighting in the auditorium had at the same time been dimmed, such that the total effect was significant enhancement of the lighting on stage. The mere fact that Lekain could call for a stage setting that was "in complete darkness" marked the new departures in lighting that had become possible.[41]

Banishment of the *petits-maîtres* meant that the stage and the auditorium had been separated into two visual worlds. If the visually spare and spartan classical theatre had in certain respects evolved in reaction to the overly complicated and cluttered *décor simultané* of the baroque theatre, so was the love of spectacle and decoration which now declared itself a reaction to the classical theatre. As a result of the isolation of the stage from the auditorium, the pendulum of stage decoration was now free to continue its swing back from whence it had come. By the end of the eighteenth century, French theatre was distinctly ready for Romanticism, with its intensified emphasis on costume, local color and elaborate historical stage settings.

Conclusion

The departure of spectators from the stage was greeted ecstatically by authors, critics and actors alike. Seemingly, the reform had everything to recommend it, and virtually no drawbacks, apart from the loss of a small amount of revenue at extremely crowded performances. One wonders, however, whether the price of order and progress on the French stage must not be reckoned by more than the few gold louis lost to the theatre troupes. No more *petits marquis* on stage meant no more frisky dogs and no more assaults on actresses. But at the same time it meant greater distance between players and public. The spectator as uninhibited quasi-participant in the spectacle was giving way to more modern modes of audience behavior: politeness, docility, remoteness—and frequently boredom. While no one can truly lament the disappearance from the French stage two centuries ago of the lacy dandies and their antics, one can nonetheless reflect that with them disappeared a certain element of spontaneity and audience involvement, the absence of which is probably still felt in the theatre today.

When in 1782 the Comédie Française installed seats in the *parterre* of its new Odéon theatre, the right of the audience to be mobile and free and move about the theatre at will—an expectation that had been brought in from the out-of-doors long before—was further curtailed. This reform served to emphasize the proscenium arch as division between active players and passive public, and to confirm the notion of the stage as a box-like room with one side missing. More recently, the stage-as-box has gone out of fashion as authors and set designers conceive of other, less rigid configurations reminiscent of an earlier time. Often the sharp line of demarcation between the area intended for the audience and that intended for the actors becomes blurred as theatre in the round, makeshift storefront theatres, street theatre and so forth gain prominence. Indeed, a few twentieth-century authors seem interested in reexploring in formal fashion that old relationship between spectators and performers. Jean Genet's *Les Nègres*, for instance, includes a contingent of actor/spectators on the stage who frequently disrupt the action. More recently,

Equus, a play that has been extremely successful in France as well as in Anglo-Saxon countries, has stage directions specifying:

> All the cast of Equus sits on Stage the entire evening. They get up to perform their Scenes, and return when they are done to their places around the set. . . . Upstage, forming a backdrop to the whole, are tiers of seats. . . . In these . . . sit members of the Audience.

The saga of the spectator on the stage, it would seem, is coming full circle.

Notes

Introduction

1. *Registre d'Hubert*, ed. Sylvie Chevalley, *Revue d'Histoire du Théâtre*, 1973, nos. 1 and 2.

2. Antoine de Léris, *Dictionnaire-portatif historique et littéraire des théâtres* (Paris: 1763; rpt. Geneva: Slatkine, 1970), p. 106.

3. (Paris: Détaille, 1875).

4. (Paris: Hachette, 1966), p. 35.

5. S. Wilma Deierkauf-Holsboer, *Histoire de la mise en scène dans le théâtre français de 1600 à 1657*, Bibliothèque de la Société des Historiens du Théâtre, I (Paris: Droz, 1933), p. 131. The author was looking at an illustration published, without any indication of its source, by Lucien Dubech, *Histoire générale illustrée du théâtre* (Paris: Librairie de France, 1932), II, p. 257. The staff at the Bibliothèque de l'Arsenal were unable to locate the original, but were in unanimous agreement that it dated from the turn of the century.

6. Wiley nearly triples the actual number of benches on the stage of that theatre. *The Hôtel de Bourgogne. Another Look at France's First Public Theatre*. Studies in Philology, vol. LXX, no. 5 (Chapel Hill: Univ. of North Carolina Press, 1973), p. 87.

7. Pierre Peyronnet, *La Mise en scène au XVIIIe siècle* (Paris: Nizet, 1974), p. 59. Emphasis in the text. This translation and the translations that follow, except where otherwise indicated, are mine.

8. These are the 1652 Gomboust plan, the Bullet plan, and the Bosse and Chauveau renderings of the interior of the Hôtel de Bourgogne, showing the stage and a portion of the audience, the whole inscribed within a circle. These are all reproduced and studied in Wiley, *Hôtel de Bourgogne*.

9. The trailblazer for these fastidious undertakings was Madame Deierkauf-Holsboer in *Le Théâtre du Marais*, 2 vols (Paris: Nizet, 1954-58), and in *Le Théâtre de l'Hôtel de Bourgogne*, 2 vols (Paris: Nizet, 1968-70). An error in Madame Deierkauf-Holsboer's calculation of the layout of the Hôtel de Bourgogne was subsequently corrected by D. H. Roy, "La Scène de l'Hôtel de Bourgogne," *Revue d'Histoire du Théâtre*, 1962, pp. 227-35. Further refinements were proposed by David V. Illingworth, "Documents inédits et nouvelles précisions sur le Théâtre de l'Hôtel de Bourgogne d'après des documents du dix-huitième siècle," *Revue d'Histoire du Théâtre*, 1970, pp. 125-32; André Villiers, "L'Ouverture de la scène à l'Hôtel de Bourgogne," *Revue d'Histoire du Théâtre*, 1970, pp. 133-41; Graham Barlow, "The Hôtel de Bourgogne According to Sir James Thornhill," *Theatre Research International*, vol. 1, no. 2 (1976), pp. 86-98; and by William L. Wiley, *Hôtel de Bourgogne*, who has tied most of the information together.

10.   *Paris Theatre Audiences in the 17th and 18th Centuries* (London: Oxford Univ. Press, 1957), p. 47.

11.   There are two annotated facsimile editions of this document. The most recent, beautifully edited by Sylvie Chevalley, is *Registre de La Grange, 1659-1685* (Genève: Minkoff, 1972). The other is edited by Bert Edward Young and Grace Philputt Young, *Le Registre de La Grange, 1659-1685* (Paris: Droz, 1947).

12.   *Le Premier Registre de la Thorillière (1663-64)*, ed. Georges Monval, (Paris: Librairie des Bibliophiles, 1890) and W. L. Schwartz, "Light on Molière in 1664 from 'Le Second Registre de La Thorillière,'" PMLA, LIII (1938), pp. 1054-75.

13.   This document has been reproduced and analyzed by Sylvie Chevalley, "Le Registre d'Hubert 1672-73," *Revue d'Histoire du Théâtre*, 1973, nos. 1 and 2. It has also been analyzed by W. L. Schwartz, "Molière's Theatre in 1672-1673: Light from Le Registre d'Hubert," PMLA, LVI (1941), pp. 395-427.

14.   These plans are reproduced, described and analyzed by Nicole Bourdel, "L'établissement et la construction de l'Hôtel des Comédiens Français, rue des Fossés-Saint-Germain-des-Prés (Ancienne Comédie) 1687-90," *Revue d'Histoire du Théâtre*, vol. 7 (1955), pp. 145-72.

15.   Jacques-François Blondel, *Architecture Française*, 4 vols. (Paris: C. A. Jombert, 1752-1756). Volume II contains plans and elevations of the Comédie Française.

16.   Gabriel-Martin Dumont, *Parallèle des plans des plus belles salles de spectacles d'Italie et de France*, (Paris, 1774 rpt. New York: B. Blom, 1968) and André-Jacob Roubo, *Traité de la construction des théâtres et des machines théâtrales* (Paris: Cellot et Jombert, 1777).

17.   Reproduced by Barlow, "The Hôtel de Bourgogne."

18.   These plans were published and analysed by Henri Lagrave, *Le Théâtre et le public à Paris de 1715 à 1750* (Paris: Klincksieck, 1972), figs. 7-12 and pp. 81-86.

19.   These records have been analysed in two master's theses: William Huss, "La Troupe de l'Hôtel Guénégaud, 1677-1680," (Paris X, 1978), and Pierre Schaffer, "Un Théâtre parisien sous Louis XIV: l'Hôtel Guénégaud de 1673 à 1677," (Paris X, 1979).

20.   MLA deposit, 523 F, 561 F and 808 F.

21.   *The Comédie Française, 1680-1701: Plays, Actors, Spectators, Finances*, Johns Hopkins Studies in Romance Literatures and Languages, ex. vol. 17 (Baltimore: The Johns Hopkins Press, 1941), and *The Comédie Française, 1701-1774*, Transactions of the American Philosophical Society, N.S. vol. 41, part 4 (Philadelphia: Am. Phil. Soc., 1951).

22.   MLA deposit, Registres de l'Opéra Comique.

23.   Henry Lyonnet, *Les Premières de Pierre Corneille* (Paris: Delagrave, 1923), p. 122.

24.   Referred to by T. E. Lawrenson, "The Shape of the 18th Century French Theatre and the Drawing Board Renaissance," *Recherches Théâtrales*, vol. VII, nos. 1-3 (1966), p. 114.

25.   T. E. Lawrenson and Helen Purkis, "Les Editions illustrées de Térence dans l'histoire du théâtre: spectacles dans un fauteuil?," in *Le Lieu théâtral à la Renaissance*, ed. Jean Jacquot (Paris: Editions du Centre national de la recherche scientifique, 1968), pp. 1-24.

26.   See my article "Cinq documents portant sur l'enceinte de la balustrade à l'Ancienne Comédie," *Revue d'Histoire du Théâtre*, 1983, pp. 174-89. The documents are also referred to in chapter 5 of this study.

27.   Edmond-Jean-François Barbier, *Chronique de la Régence et du règne de Louis XV (1718-1763)* or *Journal de Barbier* (Paris: Charpentier, 1857).

Chapter 1

1. Gustave Cohen, *L'Evolution dans la mise en scène dans le théâtre français* (Lille: Lefebvre-Ducrocq, 1910), pp. 11-12, and Simon Tidworth, *Theatres: an Illustrated History* (London: Pall Mall Press, 1973), pp. 44-45.

2. Plates I, II and III of Deierkauf-Holsboer's *Mise en scène* (1933) illustrate this.

3. Roubo, *Construction des théâtres*, pp. 26-27. Indeed, such informality could still be observed in the talking theatre as late as 1662 (see fig. 3). The figure in the left foreground is the actor Raymond Poisson as Crispin awaiting his cue. At the Opéra, the practice continued much longer. The plan representing that theatre's stage level which appears in the 1774 edition of Dumont's *Parallèle* shows a small area "J" on either side of the stage with a bench designated in the key to the plan as the "Seat for Actors on Stage" (see fig. 30).

4. H. Carrington Lancaster, *A History of French Dramatic Literature in the Seventeenth Century* (Baltimore: Johns Hopkins Press, 1929-42), III, p. 43.

5. William L. Wiley, *The Early Public Theatre in France* (Cambridge: Harvard Univ. Press, 1960), pp. 135-36.

6. Maurice Descotes, *Le public de théâtre et son histoire* (Paris: P.U.F., 1964), p. 92. Lough demonstrates that women, gentlemen, and even royalty probably attended the theatre early in the seventeenth century more than is generally acknowledged. *(Paris Theatre Audiences*, pp. 11-23.)

7. "Prologue facétieux de l'utilité du derrière," or "Avant-propos sur les tetons." *Histoire des Spectacles*, ed. Guy Dumur, Encyclopédie de la Pléiade (Paris: N.R.F., 1965), pp. 749-50. Pierre-David Lemazurier, *Galérie historique des acteurs du théâtre français, depuis 1600 jusqu'à nos jours* (Paris: Chaumerot, 1810), I, pp. 26-27.

8. Wiley, *Early Public Theatre*, pp. 55-57.

9. Descotes, *Le public de théâtre*, p. 192 for citation; S. Wilma Deierkauf-Holsboer, *Histoire de la mise en scène dans le Théâtre Français, à Paris, de 1600 à 1673* (Paris: Nizet, 1960), p. 19.

10. Georges Mongrédien, *Les Grands comédiens au XVIIe siècle* (Paris: Le Livre, 1927), p. 46.

11. From the publisher's preface "Au lecteur," cited by Lancaster, *History*, II, p. 360. Lancaster believes that the play, published in 1642, was probably first acted in 1640 at the Palais Cardinal, predecessor to the Palais Royal.

12. Cited by Lancaster, *History*, III, p. 43.

13. Cited by Deierkauf-Holsboer, *Mise en scène* (1960), p. 268, from the *Epitre dédicatoire à Guillemette* (1648).

14. Information drawn from Wiley, *Early Public Threatre*, pp. 55-57; Deierkauf-Holsboer, *Hôtel de Bourgogne*, II, p. 57 and *Mise en scène* (1960), p. 19.

15. This well known passage from the *Historiettes* is cited by, among others, Pierre Melèse in *Le Théâtre et le public à Paris sous Louis XIV (1639-1713)* (Paris: Droz, 1934), p. 211.

16. A remark in the preface of a 1660 play by F. Donneau, cited by John Lough in *Paris Theatre Audiences*, p. 63.

17. The presence of marquis on the stage of the Palais Royal is referred to in 1663 in De Visé's *Réponse à l'Impromptu*, a play designed to attack Molière and defend the marquis. A character in De Visé's play, who has just seen *l'Impromptu de Versailles* at the Palais Royal,

comments on the spectators on the stage and on the actor who ridiculed them (i.e., Molière himself): "in truth, a Marquis is a fine thing. I was shown several nearby the person who was imitating them, and I couldn't imagine how he dared make fun of them . . . " (I, iii).

18. *Fâch.* I, i; *Crit.* v; *Mis.* III, i.

19. An additional instance in which Molière ridiculed this type of spectator is indicated by a 1665 entry in the *Registre de La Grange:* "Friday 12 June, upon the King's order, the troupe went to Versailles where we gave the favorite show in the Garden on a Stage all decorated with orange trees. Mr. de Molière did a prologue as a Ridiculous marquis who wanted to be on the Stage despite the guards and [he] had a ludicrous conversation with an actress sitting in the middle of the audience playing the Ridiculous marquise." (Young and Young, p. 76.)

20. The engraving was found by A. Ross Curtis, who reproduced it and commented upon it in "A propos d'une gravure de 1662," *Revue d'Histoire du Théâtre,* 1967, pp. 97-98. The original, the frontispiece to Poisson's play, is held by the Bibliothèque de l'Arsenal, Rf 6668.

21. The play, *Les Amours de Calotin,* by Chevalier, is referred to by Lancaster, *History,* III, p. 327.

22. Molière's troupe undertook to "refurbish all the *loges* and amphitheatre, benches and *balcons.*" Young and Young, *Registre de La Grange,* I, p. 124.

23. First cited by Eugène Despois, *Le Théâtre français sous Louis XIV* (Paris: Hachette, 1874), p. 118, note 3.

24. III, i. Cited by Lough in *Paris Theatre Audiences,* p. 117.

25. First cited by Despois in *Le Théâtre français,* p. 118.

26. This remark from the *Mercure* of May 23, 1759, is cited by Despois in *Le Théâtre français,* p. 129.

Chapter 2

1. Lagrave, *Public,* pp. 262-85.

2. Lough, *Background,* p. 58 and Lancaster, *History,* I, pp. 713-14.

3. Lough, *Background,* pp. 61-63 and Wiley, *Early Public Theatre,* p. 202.

4. This innovation at the Opéra is described by Lagrave, *Public,* p. 82. Lough, in calling the Ancienne Comédie Paris's "first theatre in which the auditorium was shaped in the form of an ellipse" *(Background,* p. 59), overlooks what had been done at the Palais Royal more than a decade earlier.

5. These and other relevant documents are published and analyzed in my article about the balustrade referred to in the Introduction. In addition to the Le Pautre engraving, visual material pertaining to the subject consists of a 1726 engraving by Coypel (fig. 40) and a later plan and elevation of the Comédie Française appearing in Blondel's *Architecture Française* (figs. 8 and 9). In addition, a good description of the *enceinte de la balustrade* as it had become by the middle of the century appears in Barbier's *Journal,* vol. VII, pp. 161-63.

6. Jean Nicolas Du Tralage, *Mélanges sur la comédie et l'opéra.* Excerpts from a collection of Du Tralage manuscripts are published in *Notes et Documents sur l'histoire des théâtres de Paris,* ed. Jacob (Paris: Librairie des bibliophiles, 1880). The passage (pp. 85-86) dates from 1695, but since Lully died in 1687, one must suppose that what is described took place before then.

7. Cited by Melèse, *Le Théâtre et le public.* p. 64. The *filles de l'Opéra* were, of course, noted for their beauty and availability.

8. Ibid.

9. First cited by Despois in *Le Théâtre français,* pp. 120-21.

10. Lagrave, in his accounting of the capacity of the Comédie Italienne, does not include spectators on the stage *(Public,* p. 89).

11. Pp. 61-62.

12. First cited by Despois in *Le Théâtre français,* pp. 120-21.

13. May 18, 1716; Bibliothèque Historique de la Ville de Paris, 138 450 t. 22, no. 46. Peyronnet, looking at entries in the *Registres du Théâtre Italien,* concludes that because "teatri" tickets were not always noted, stage seats "were not regularly rented" (p. 59, n. 171). Closer study suggests that omission or inclusion of this notation varied according to the *semainier* who happened to be keeping the books (Paghetti, for instance, was more meticulous than Alborghetti), and that stage seats were rented regularly, not sporadically.

14. The report was written by the Commissaire Daminois. Cited by Lagrave, *Public,* p. 101, from Campardon.

15. Lagrave, *Public,* p. 98, drawing from the same source as above.

16. Cited by Lagrave, *Public,* p. 101, n. 97. The play premiered at the Foire Saint Germain on March 27, 1716.

17. Bibliothèque Historique de la Ville de Paris, N.F. 35 380 t. 136 no. 25; and 138 450 vol. 33, no. 4.

18. Many of these ordinances can be read in Nicolas de Lamare, *Moeurs,* 1893 (Bibliothèque Nationale, Salle des Manuscrits, Fonds de la Mare, ff 21625).

19. Jean-Marie-Bernard Clément and Abbé Jean-Barthélemy de la Porte, *Anecdotes dramatiques* (Paris: Vve Duchesne, 1775), I, 4-5.

20. Dumont, *Parallèle.*

21. C. J. Gossip, "Le Décor de théâtre au collège des Jésuites à Paris au XVIIe siècle," *Revue d'Histoire du Théâtre* 1981, p. 36.

Chapter 3

1. The drawing, in india ink, is held by the Service des plans, cartes et dessins of the Archives Nationales (call number O'3238, fol. 32). Certain characteristics of the drawing, and of some companion drawings, suggest that it is part of a proposal for construction or remodeling of a theatre. The theatre in question has not been identified.

2. Cited by Jullien, in *Le Spectateur,* p. 26.

3. Frédéric Deloffre, in his introduction to Marivaux's *Petit-maître corrigé* (Geneva: Droz, 1955), pp. 19-23.

4. Cited by Alfred Franklin, *La Vie privée d'autrefois: arts, et métiers, modes, moeurs, usages des Parisiens, du XIIe au XVIIIe siècle.* (Paris: Plon et Nourrit, 1898), XXI, p. 47. The title page of the guidebook is also reproduced by Franklin. Written by one J. S. Nemeitz, advisor to the Prince de Waldeck, its full title is *Séjour de Paris, c'est à dire, Instructions fidèles, pour les Voiageurs de Condition, Comment ils se doivent conduire, s'ils veulent faire un bon usage de leur tems & argent, durant leur Séjour à Paris.*

5. Most of the observations in this paragraph are based on Lagrave, *Public,* pp. 417-30.

6. Cited by Lagrave, *Public,* p. 418.

7. Blondel, *Architecture Française,* II, p. 33.

8. Jules Bonnassies, *La Comédie Française. Notice historique sur les anciens bâtiments* (Paris: Aubry, 1868), pp. 21-22.

9. Cited by Lagrave, *Public,* p. 419.

10. An entry for November 24, 1700 in *Les pièces et rapports de police manuscrits* (Bibliothèque Nationale), cited by Jules Bonnassies, *La Comédie Française. Histoire administrative, 1658-1757.* (Paris: Didier, 1874), pp. 331-32.

11. Cited by Lagrave, *Public,* p. 420.

12. Cited by Claude Alasseur, *La Comédie Française au 18e siècle: étude économique* (Paris: Mouton, 1967), p. 13.

13. Cited by Lough, *Background,* p. 124, from Palaprat's *Discours sur le Grondeur.*

14. Charles de Fieux, chevalier de Mouhy, *Abrégé de l'histoire du Théâtre Français depuis son origine jusqu'au premier juin 1780* (Paris: L. Jorry, 1780-1783), III, pp. 31-32. The incident is also recounted in Clément and de la Porte, *Anecdotes dramatiques,* II, pp. 20-21.

15. See Franklin L. Ford, *Robe and Sword: The Regrouping of the French Aristocracy after Louis XIV* (New York: Harper and Row, 1953), pp. 207ff. According to Ford, "Between 1732 and 1748, in the Paris area alone, there were 1,207 payments of finances for ennoblement or confirmation...."

16. See Richard Sennett, *The Fall of Public Man* (New York: Vintage Books-Random House, 1978), pp. 76-77.

17. Lemazurier, *Galérie,* I, pp. 195-96. Mademoiselle Dumesnil first appeared on the stage of the Comédie Française in 1737.

18. P. 282.

19. Mouhy, *Abrégé,* III, p. 31. Mouhy refers to the play as *Gentilhomme Crispin,* but there was no such play. According to Lancaster, *History,* III, p. 839, the play was performed at the Marais Theatre.

20. Pierre-Jacques Brillon, *Le Théophraste modèrne, ou Nouveaux caractères des moeurs* (Paris: Brunet, 1701), p. 422.

21. Cited by Lagrave, *Public,* p. 420.

22. Clément and de la Porte, *Anecdotes dramatiques,* I, 1-2. The play in question was *Abdilly, Roi de Grenade,* by M. de l'Isle and Mlle. Riccoboni.

23. Ludovic Leclerc (Celler), *Les Décors, les costumes et la mise en scène au XVIIe siècle (1615-1680),* (1869; rpt. Geneva: Slatkine, 1970), p. 142.

24. *Feuille d'assemblée* for May 6, 1697; Archives of the Comédie Française.

25. Cited by Lagrave, *Public,* p. 222, from a manuscript in the Bibliothèque de l'Arsenal, *Anecdotes de l'Opéra-Comique.*

26. Lough, *Background,* p. 125; Alasseur, *Comédie,* p. 11; and Melèse, *Théâtre,* p. 210.

27. Lancaster notes that prices were frequently doubled at the Comédie Française when French and foreign royalty and nobility were in attendance. *(Comédie Française, 1701-74, p. 594.)*

28. Riccoboni's *Réflexions historiques,* 1738, cited by Lough, *Background,* p. 229.

29. Cited by Melèse, *Théâtre,* p. 212. Figures published by Lancaster in *Comédie Française, 1680-1701* confirm that *Judith* was indeed very well attended during its early performances in March 1695.

30. First cited by Despois, *Le Théâtre français,* p. 119. It should be noted that Lesage's account did not appear until 1740 (in *La Valise trouvée),* nearly a half-century after the fact. While there were frequently two hundred spectators on the stage in 1740, this was not necessarily so in 1695.

31. Although the first performance of the *Judith* on March 4 did not attract an outstandingly large crowd in the expensive seats—only one lower box and 152 tickets at three *livres* were sold—the play seems to have caught on, starting with the second performance. While not many full boxes were rented for the next several performances, sales of three-*livre* tickets rose as high as 292. Not all of these were necessarily for stage seats, since lower box tickets were the same price. (Figures obtained from microfilms of the *Registres* held by the Library of Congress, MLA, 561F.)

32. August 1721, p. 102.

33. The *Princesse de Navarre* was given as part of the festival in honor of the Dauphin's first marriage. It was performed to overflow crowds in the indoor riding ring of the *grande écurie,* converted to a theatre (Lagrave, *Public,* pp. 156-60).

34. Bonnassies, who perused documents in the Archives of the Comédie Française, states that "The stage boxes are reserved for important lords (as well as important ladies) who are intimates of the troupe." *Bâtiments,* p. 21.

35. The *feuille d'assemblée* of the Comédie Française for August 21, 1690, records that "It has been decided that no domestic will be admitted to anywhere but the third tier of stage boxes...and that to this end the actors and actresses will have one key per household." The September 18 entry reports that "keys for the doors to the stage boxes" were made and distributed to the actors and actresses. *(Feuilles d'assemblée,* Archives of the Comédie Française.)

36. Cited by Lagrave, *Public,* p. 424.

37. Claude-Gilbert Dubois, *Le Baroque: profondeurs de l'apparence* (Paris: Librairie Larousse, 1973), pp. 159-97.

38. The historical importance of clothing as the most reliable indicator of social class is, of course, attested to by the exquisite precision of the sumptuary laws. Some of the reasons for which the *petits marquis,* so many of them newly arrived, might have been particularly prone to cling to such symbols of social status, in the face of the demographic changes that were taking place in the eighteenth century, are suggested by Richard Sennett, *Fall.*

39. See Alexandre Cianorescu, "Baroque et action dramatique: le dehors et le dedans," in *Le Baroque au théâtre et la théâtralité du Baroque* (Montauban: CNRS, 1967), pp. 100-3.

Chapter 4

1. Regarding Donneau de Visé, Young and Young say that "it is known that this man of many pursuits was rather intimately acquainted with Molière's troupe, and that he performed some unspecified duties for the benefit of the Company ... " (II, p. 114). Sylvie Chevalley observes that "it was probably as a special favor that Molière authorized 36 spectators on the stage. For his own plays, even on the best days, the number of spectators is 32." *(Registre d'Hubert,* p. 165, n. 50.)

2. That number of stage tickets was sold twice before Molière's death (at the opening of *Psyché,* and at a performance of the *Malade imaginaire),* and seven times after his death (again for the *Malade imaginaire).*

3. The plays in question are listed in a note to table I.

4. *Entrées gratuites* are discussed below.

5. II, p. 33. According to Blondel's *Architecture Française,* these boxes were known as *balcons* because they were located directly above the *balcons* or balustrades behind which the stage benches were enclosed. The wrought iron construction of the balustrades was doubtless very similar to that which was used for balconies outside windows.

6. Lancaster felt that *balcons* were probably introduced in 1682, but he was doubtless unaware of the 1677 mention. *(History,* IV, p. 42.)

7. .For twenty-six performances of *Andromède,* the sale of *balcon* tickets was recorded separately from that of other categories of tickets. The figures of one hundred and eighty appear on the registers for January 24 and 29, 1683, respectively.

8. Dividing 33 £ (the price for rental of an entire stage box or *loge de balcon)* by 5 £ 10s yields six places; by the same token, 44 £ (the price of a regular *loge)* divided by 5 £ 10s yields eight places.

9. This configuration is proposed by Lagrave, *Public,* p. 76. Interpreting the Blondel plans, Lagrave suggests that the twelve *balcons* consisted of six boxes holding eight persons, and six holding ten persons, for a total of 108 places *(Public,* p. 80).

10. According to Lagrave, the number of spectators per box "can rise, under exceptional circumstances, to an astonishing number: the Parfaict Brothers state ... that during a free performance given August 8, 1721 at the Comédie Française, there were counted 'as many as 14 persons in a single box.'!" *(Public,* p. 105, n. 3). The *Mercure de France* reported that for a gratis performance at the Opéra in November 1728 there were sixteen persons in most of the *loges* meant for eight, while on the same day the Comédie Française squeezed in twenty. (Lagrave, *Public,* p. 215). And, for a gratis performance of Du Belloy's *Siège de Calais* on March 12, 1765 for the people of the Halles, an eyewitness reports that "the boxes, which are only meant for eight persons, contained fifteen or sixteen, one on top of the other" (Cited by H. C. Lancaster, *Sunset, A History of Parisian Drama in the Last Years of Louis XIV, 1701-1715* [Baltimore: Johns Hopkins Press, 1945], p. 484).

11. The existence of this scale, now presumably hidden under the frame, was noted by Bapst, who examined the entire drawing (Noëlle Guibert, "La Place du décor dans le théâtre du XVIIe siècle en France," *Comédie Française,* No. 94 [1980], p. 37, n. 17). The framed sketch is on display at the Archives of the Comédie Française. In contrast to Bapst's assurances, Chappuzeau, talking about the newly formed Troupe du Roy (1673), states that "it possesses very fine quarters, with a stage wide enough and deep enough for the largest machines" (Samuel Chappuzeau, *Le Théâtre Français, divisé en trois livres, où il est traité de l'usage de la Comédie, des auteurs qui soutiennent le théâtre, de la conduite des comédiens* [Paris, 1674; rpt. Paris: J. Bonnassies, 1876], p. 121).

12. Lancaster, *Histoire*. IV, pp. 260 and 567.

13. An analysis of some of the data in these registers and a detailed discussion of *balcons* can be found in my article, "Les Spectateurs sur la scène: quelques chiffres tirés des registres du XVIIe siècle," *Revue d'Histoire du Théâtre*, 1980, pp. 199-215. Despite these very elevated numbers, it is not likely that permanent seating on the stage was augmented at this time. (See below, 1715-16 evidence showing two *gradins* only.)

14. Consulting the 1688 bylaws of the Comédie Française, Alasseur counted 103 exemptions (p. 31). The bylaws and the list of exemptions appear in Bonnassies, *Hist. admin.*, pp. 111-17. For the eighteenth century, Lagrave estimates about five hundred authorized exemptions (*Public*, p. 183). An admirably detailed discussion of the question of the non-paying spectator is presented by Lagrave, pp. 175-85.

15. Lagrave, *Public*, p. 184.

16. Bonnassies, *Hist. admin.*, p. 111.

17. Lagrave, *Public*, p. 184, n. 34.

18. Cf. Barbier's testimony cited below, and Le Pautre's series of *Noce de village* engravings.

19. Blondel, *Architecture Française*, II, p. 31. Indeed, the records frequently indicate few, if any, paid admissions to the amphitheatre.

20. Information in this paragraph is based on my article, "Cinq documents."

21. Sometimes tickets to the amphitheatre were pegged at the same price as stage seats or the best box seats. However, according to Lancaster, *Comédie Française, 1680-1701*, p. 17, the amphitheatre "was usually empty of spectators who paid." That is, that part of the auditorium was mostly used to accommodate spectators entitled to enter without paying, and so the present calculations should not be much affected by the inclusion of the few amphitheatre tickets that might have been sold. When considering records dating from about 1710 onward, account must be taken of forty orchestra seats, usually priced the same as stage seats.

22. Lancaster states that "there could be no performance because the audience objected to an announcement made by Dancourt" (*Comédie Française, 1680-1701*, p. 2).

23. The notation "théâtre" appears alongside the December 14 entry of the 5 £ 12s tickets, such that it can be safely assumed that the other entries at that price are also for stage seats.

24. Lancaster states that in 1693 *Andromède* played twelve times at the Comédie Française, (*History*, II, 682), but this is an error. Lancaster's own listing of performances shows 1683 as the last year *Andromède* was performed at that theatre.

25. Blondel, *Architecture Française*, II, p. 33.

26. *Rapports inédits du Lieutenant de police René d'Argenson, 1697-1715*, ed. Paul Cottin, in Bibliothèque Elzévirienne (Paris: E. Plon, Nourrit et Cie, 1891), p. 357.

27. Archives of the Comédie Française, Carton 151.

28. Paul Poisson had resigned from the troupe in 1711, and began playing in fair theatres. Upon Louis XIV's death, when the Regent took over control of the theatre, his daughter, the Duchesse de Berry, persuaded Paul and his son Philippe to return to the Comédie Française. (Lancaster, *Sunset*, pp. 13 and 335).

29. The dimensions are given by Blondel, *Architecture Française*, II, p. 33, and the seating capacity of the stage has been calculated by Lagrave, *Public*, pp. 79-81.

30. Barbier. *Journal,* VII. pp. 161-62.

31. The number calculated by Lagrave, *Public,* p. 81.

32. Further narrative confirmation appears in an account written by Lesage in 1740 *(La Valise trouvée)*. Focussing on the novelty of women sitting on the stage some years earlier, Lesage refers to "two hundred ladies seated on benches." (Cited by Lough, *Background,* p. 115).

33. To the 140 places of the permanent benches. I have added 28 places for the extra benches (Lagrave calculates 14 places for the first bench inside the balustrade so I have assumed the same for the bench just outside the balustrade), for a total of 218. When one adds the 108 seats in the stage boxes, as calculated by Lagrave, one arrives at the grand total.

34. *Feuille d'assemblée* for March 20. 1698 (Archives of the Comédie Française).

35. Lyonnet. *Premières,* p. 119. According to Alasseur, *Comédie,* p. 76, the cheapest tickets cost the equivalent of a day's manual labor, and the most expensive equaled forty to fifty days of labor.

36. Du Tralage, *Mélanges,* p. 62.

37. Riccoboni, *Reflexions,* p. 134.

38. Statements about Hôtel Guénégaud prices are based on my own perusal of the *registres* for 1673-1679. Statements about Comédie Française prices are based on Alasseur's table, "Prix des places à la Comédie Française (1680-1782)." *Comédie,* p. 77.

39. Lagrave, *Public,* p. 50. The term derived from the fact that the increment was equivalent to one-third of the increased price. Thus the normal four-*livre* ticket would be raised to six *livres,* a policy that the Comédie Française had already been trying out since 1730.

40. H.C. Lancaster, *French Tragedy in the Time of Louis XV and Voltaire, 1715-1774* (Baltimore: Johns Hopkins Press, 1950), p. 8.

41. Lancaster, *Comédie Française, 1701-1774,* pp. 594 and 629.

42. Alasseur, *Comédie,* p. 11.

43. Lancaster, *Louis XV,* p. 8.

44. Chevalley calculates a theoretical capacity of 1,057 at the Palais Royal, though this number of paid admissions was never attained. (*Registre d'Hubert,* pp. 166-68).

45. Lagrave, *Public,* p. 81.

46. Sixteen of the twenty-four lower boxes *(loges basses)* were sold as units, leaving eight for which individual seats could be sold. Those 64 tickets, added to 40 for orchestra seats, amount to 104 of the 437 tickets sold at six *livres*. Performing the subtraction, we are left with 233 tickets for spectators on the stage.

Chapter 5

1. Germain Bapst, *Essai sur l'histoire du théâtre, la mise en scène, le décor, le costume, l'architecture, l'éclairage, l'hygiène* (Paris: Lahure, 1893), p. 373.

2. Bibliothèque Nationale, Cabinet des Estampes, Ed 42a.

3. The scene from *Cinna* is a vignette within an allegorical representation of La Poésie which appeared in *Le Cabinet des beaux-arts* by Charles Perrault (Paris: G. Edelinck, 1690). Pierre

Le Pautre based his engraving on a painting by Alexandre, which must have been executed some years earlier. (Julien Alexandre, the only painter by that name working in the last half of the seventeenth century, was born in 1653 and died in 1679.) The depiction of stage boxes suggests the Hôtel Guénégaud, probably the only theatre to have such boxes at the time. Le Pautre's engraving was reproduced by Jacques Vanuxem in "Le Décor de théâtre sous Louis XIV," *Dix-Septième Siècle*, No. 39 (1958), p. 209. A curious mirror image of the *Cinna* scene appears in an engraving entitled "Melpomène" by H. Bonnart, in a series on the nine Muses. (Bibliothèque Nationale, Cabinet des Estampes, Oa 78 pet.fol., p. 41) (fig. 21).

4. Bourdel, "L'établissement." At the Bibliothèque Nationale there is a curious, and as yet unauthenticated, plan entitled "Second plan des 1ères loges." Very similar to the d'Orbay plan, it has had added to it a rough pencil sketch of a balustrade and orchestra seating. (Cabinet des Estampes, Topographie de Paris, VIe arr. 21ème quartier, Va 263) (fig. 22).

5. Ordinarily the troupe held assembly on Mondays, a custom observed since 31 August 1682, according to La Grange's register. (Young and Young, I, p. 299.)

6. This *procuration*, as well as the *marché* (contract) cited below, and a *quittance*, (receipt) all pertaining to the balustrade, are held by the Minutier Central, VI, p. 589.

7. A *toise* was equal to six *pieds*. In terms of modern measurements, a *toise* is the equivalent of seventy-six inches, or 1.949 meters.

8. This account book, entitled "Dépenses de l'Etablissement par Monsieur de la Grange—20 juin 1687 au 17 novembre 1691," is held by the Archives of the Comédie Française, carton 171. The pages having to do with the balustrade were kindly made available to me by Mme Sylvie Chevalley, who is preparing an edition of the document. The two pages (99 and 100) are transcribed and analyzed in my article "Cinq documents."

9. Archives of the Comédie Française.

10. This transcription of *règlements intérieurs* passed in 1697 appears in Bonnassies, *Hist. admin.*, p. 125.

11. Bonnassies, *Hist. admin.*, p. 122. The item concerning control of non-paying spectators appeared routinely in Comédie Française bylaws. Installation of a *cloison forte*, however, was not proposed until 1697. It would be tempting to assume that the need for a special partition at the Comédie Française was related to additional traffic resulting from the ouster of the Comédie Italienne from Paris that same year. This, however, does not appear to have been the case: drafting of the 1697 bylaws was completed on 22 April (Bonnassies, *Hist. admin.*, p. 110), whereas the Comédie Italienne was not ordered into exile until 13 May.

12. Barbier, *Journal*, VII, p. 163. Though written in 1759, this description was meant to reflect a long-standing situation which, in Barbier's words, existed "depuis toujours."

13. Lagrave, *Public*, p. 655.

14. Although I have not been able to find a copy of that ordinance, its existence is attested to by a subsequent letter from Pontchartrain deploring the fact that "good order on the premises of the theatres" has not been maintained "since the time [His Majesty] gave orders for extension of the balustrade on the stage of the Comédie." (Bibliothèque Nationale, Salle des Manuscrits, ff9236, p. 84.) The letter, written in 1713, will be discussed below.

15. The decision to undertake inspection of the boxes is entered on the *feuille d'assemblée* for December 26, 1689, while the resolution to avoid further indecency in the third balconies is part of the *feuille d'assemblée* for March 9, 1693.

16. "The Opéra and the two Comédies each had their surveillant, responsible for maintaining order and decency, an uneasy task which in the end was much better performed by the loaded guns of the national guard." Marc Chassaigne, *La Lieutenance générale de police de Paris* (1906; rpt., Geneva: Slatkine-Megariotis, 1975), p. 194.

17. The functions and relationship of these two officials is explained by Cottin, *Rapports inédits*, pp. vi–vii. "The position of lieutenant of police at the end of the reign of Louis XIV was almost that of a minister, given the extent to which he enjoyed the king's confidence. The *Rapports* ... are addressed to the minister under whose jurisdiction Paris fell, that is, Count Jérôme de Pontchartrain, son of the chancellor.... Jérôme Phélypeaux, like his father, bore the title of Count of Pontchartrain...."

18. Bibliothèque Nationale, Salle des Manuscrits, ff9236, p. 84. The letter is dated November 28.

19. Ibid.

20. Ibid.

21. Ibid., p. 83, letter dated December 21.

22. *Rapports inédits*, p. 357.

23. Barbier, *Journal*, as previously cited.

24. Cited by Lagrave, *Public*, p. 111.

25. Cited by Lagrave, *Public*, p. 111, n. 21. Policy regarding differentiation of tickets must have varied over the years. A printer's bill covering the year 1714 shows that the troupe ordered *billets de théâtre* several times: "on May 12 furnished 400 *billets de théâtre* in two colors at the agreed on price of thirty sous the hundred, total six *livres*," etc. (Memoire des Impressions, Archives of the Comédie Française, 1715 folder).

26. The *feuilles d'assemblée* and the *facture* are part of the collection of the Archives de la Comédie Française.

27. Bibliothèque Historique de la Ville de Paris, 138 450 t.22, no.46.

28. Barlow, "The Hôtel de Bourgogne." Mr. Barlow does not mention the balustrades in his article; however, when this interpretation of the sketch was pointed out to him in private correspondence, he agreed that a balustrade was indeed depicted.

29. A. J.-B. d'Origny, *Annales du Théâtre Italien depuis son origine jusqu'à ce jour* (Paris: Vve Duchesne, 1768), I, p. 296.

30. Bibliothèque Historique de la Ville de Paris, N.F. 35 380, t.117, no.65.

31. I have found ordinances referring specifically to the stage, as distinguished from ordinances having to do with general misconduct in theatres, for the following dates: May 18, 1716; April 10, 1720; November 16, 1720; November 24, 1722; January 11, 1725; June 22, 1725; January 17, 1726; January 23, 1728; July 20, 1728; December 7, 1728; February 1, 1739; January 20, 1741; January 12, 1742; January 15, 1742; February 2, 1745; April 10, 1747; May 7, 1749; April 25, 1751; November 29, 1757. These ordinances can be read variously at the Bibliothèque Nationale, Salle des Manuscrits (Fonds de la Mare, ff21625, pp. 243, 245, 247, 248, 249, 252, 254, 256, 258 and 337) and at the Bibliothèque Historique de la Ville de Paris (138 450: t.22, no.46; t.33, no.4; t.73, no.74 and N.F. 35 380; t.115, no.14; t.117, no.65; t.136, no.25; t.170, no.41; t.174, no.62 and t.172, no.31).

32. Reiterated was the prohibition "to all persons against stopping in the wings which serve as entrance to the stages of the two Comédies, and outside the balustrades which are installed there." (Bibliothèque Historique, N.F. 35 380: t.175, no.176.)

33. The 1769 ordinance, dated December 24, is reproduced in Des Essarts, dit Nicolas-Toussaint le Moyne, *Les trois théâtres de Paris, ou Abrégé historique de l'établissement de la Comédie Française, de la Comédie Italienne et de l'Opéra* (Paris: Lacombe, 1777), pp. 150-51. It is always possible that a typographical error crept into the reproduction of the date of this ordinance. It is more likely, however, that royal printers, when directed to produce a new batch of theatre ordinances, merely pulled out an old bed of type, changed the date, and proceeded to reprint without rereading. This supposition is supported by the fact that although the Comédie Italienne was banned from Paris between 1697 and 1716, ordinances issued on February 12, 1698, November 11, 1699 and April 11, 1701 all refer to that troupe. (Bibliothèque Nationale, Réserve, G.F. 15(217)1698, and Salle des Manuscrits, Fond de la Mare, ff21625, pp. 241-42.)

Chapter 6

1. Du Tralage, *Mélanges*, p. 87.

2. Cited by Mélèse, *Théâtre*, p. 64. To be sure, Dufresny's *Amusements sérieux et comiques* published in 1699 contains an anecdote about spectators on the stage of the Opéra (cited in an earlier chapter), but this discrepancy can be attributed to the normal time lag between writing and publication.

3. Cited by Lagrave, *Public*, p. 84.

4. Luigi Riccoboni, *Réflexions historiques et critiques sur les différents théâtres de l'Europe* (Paris: J. Guérin, 1738), p. 140.

5. Blondel, *Architecture Française*, II, p. 33.

6. Cited by Jullien, *Le Spectateur*, p. 17.

7. 1760, p. 54.

8. Charles Collé, *Journal et mémoires*, ed. H. Bonhomme (Paris: Didot, 1868), I, pp. 2-3.

9. *Mémoires*, cited by Jullien, in *Le Spectateur*, pp. 17-18. The attendance figure is from Lancaster, *Louis XV*, p. 336.

10. Cited by Lancaster, *Louis XV*, p. 336. A similar outburst in which the cry was "Make way for the mailman" ("Place au facteur") has been recounted in the introductory section of this study. The occasion was the premiere of Morand's *Childéric* on December 19, 1736. The implication that attendance was very heavy at these events is borne out by the records. The first performance of *Childéric* drew 951 paid admissions, the highest number for the season. At the premiere of *Sémiramis* on August 29, 1748, there were 1,117 paid admissions, tied with another play for the record high of that season.

11. Cited by Jullien, *Le Spectateur*, p. 18.

12. Collé, I, *Journal*, p. 3.

13. Cited by Jullien, *Le Spectateur*, p. 18.

14. Cited by Lagrave, *Public*, pp. 110-11, from the *Mercure de France* for June 1750, II, p. 141.

15. Information about this incident is taken from: P. Berret, "Comment la scène française du XVIIIe siècle a été débarassée de la présence des gentilshommes," *Revue d'histoire littéraire*, 1901, pp. 456-59; Duc de Luynes, *Mémoires sur la Cour de Louis XV, 1735-1738*, (Paris: Firmin-Didot, 1860-1865), XI, pp. 113 and 133-34; Collé, *Journal*, I, pp. 380-81; Bonnassies, *Hist. admin.*, p. 105; and *Bâtiments*, p. 23.

16. Albert Babeau explains that "Since nobles were not admitted to the stage at the Opéra, the *petites loges* fronting on the stage . . . had multiplied" *(Le Théâtre des Tuileries sous Louis XIV, Louis XV et Louis XVI,* [Nogent-le-Rotrou: Daupeley-Gouverneur, 1895], p. 29). Lagrave states that "Installed on either side of the stage, they were rented by the year, at quite variable rates; despite their miniscule dimensions and their discomfort, they were much sought after by faithful Opéra-goers." *(Public,* p. 84.) In a note, Lagrave cites a 1723 letter from Voltaire to Mme de Bernières on the subject: "For 400 francs at most, and probably for one hundred *écus,* you can have the *petite loge* you are requesting for the winter" (*Public,* p. 84, n. 37.) Lagrave further shows that *petites loges* existed at the Opéra as early as 1718 (p. 210). That arrangement, incidentally, endured into our own century until January of 1914 at which time "the Opera eliminated boxes on the stage." Lyonnet, *Les Premières,* p. 61.

17. The Duc de Luynes, as cited by Berret, in "Comment la scène," pp. 458-59. In his *Mémoires,* this personage further states that "La Noue, an actor, was put in prison by order of the First Gentleman of the King's Bed Chamber, because of construction of boxes at the Comédie" (p. 133).

18. The Gentlemen of the King's Bed Chamber had responsibility for and control of the royal theatres. Troupe members were obliged to put up with the Gentlemen's capricious behavior, orders and counter-orders, relative to acceptance or rejection of new actors, new plays and so forth. On November 14, 1757 the Comédie Française voted to rebuild the six *petites loges* in the first wing openings, and to install four more at the back of the amphitheatre. In addition to these ten newly-constructed boxes, the *troisièmes loges* (third tier of boxes) were also designated as *petites loges.* (Normal size boxes were no doubt subdivided and provided with fuller partitions for greater privacy as depicted in the P.A. Wille drawing of the Hôtel de Bourgogne, figure 37.) This time the installation was authorized by royal authority. Hoping to give the troupe a financial boost, the king granted permission to rent these and certain other boxes on a yearly or even a lifetime basis *(loges à vie),* at 3,000 *livres* each, with tax-exempt status. Despite their ad hoc nature, these *loges* constituted a very important source of income for the troupe, accounting over the years for about one-third of the total. (Alasseur, *Comédie,* pp. 10 and 71; Lancaster, *Louis XV,* pp. 4-5 and 8; Bonnassies, *Bâtiments,* p. 18; *Almanach des spectacles,* 1757, p. 52.)

19. Cited by Lancaster, *Louis XV,* p. 245. The play was first performed January 12, 1739. The problem of spectators on the stage must have been perceived as particularly onerous in 1739. Mouhy's *Tablettes dramatiques* report that "there were so many people on the stage at the performance of *Athalie,* the 16 December 1739, and the *parterre* was so excessively full and so tumultuous, that the players could not finish the play" (cited by Lagrave, *Public,* p. 79 and by Jullien, *Le Spectateur,* p. 9). Unfortunately the *registres* for 1739-40 are lost and so Mouhy's account cannot be verified.

20. Denis Diderot, *Correspondance,* ed. Georges Roth (Paris: Editions de Minuit, 1956), II, pp. 89-90 (November 27, 1758).

21. Lancaster, *Louis XV,* p. 471 and Pierre Laurent De Belloy, *Oeuvres complètes,* (Paris: Moutard, 1779), I, pp. 176-77.

22. In his edition of Lekain's *Mémoires,* Talma notes that "The advantage that the public would enjoy from the modifications proposed by Lekain was incontestable, but it was necessary to buy it by sacrificing a portion of the boxoffice, and that consideration held back the Comédie." Henry Louis Cain Lekain, *Mémoires de Lekain, précédés de réflexions sur cet acteur, et sur l'art théâtral,* ed. Talma (Paris; 1825: rpt. Genève Slatkine, 1968), p. 147, n. 1.

23. According to Peyronnet, *La Mise en scène,* p. 100, the two plays were *Iphigénie en Tauride* and *Colère d'Achille,* neither of which were ever to be accepted by the Comédie Française.

24. The French title of Lekain's memorandum was: "Mémoire qui tend à prouver la nécessité de supprimer les banquettes de dessus le théâtre de la Comédie-Française, en séparant ainsi les acteurs des spectateurs." Information about Lekain's role in this matter is based on Jean-Jacques Olivier, *Henri-Louis Le Kain de la Comédie-Française (1729-1778)* (Paris: Soc. française d'Imprimerie et de Librairie, 1907), pp. 168-70, and Talma/ Lekain, pp. 135-48. All citations from Lekain's *Mémoires* are from those pages.

25. Information about cost is from Collé, *Journal*, II, pp. 274-75 and P. Fromageot, "Les Fantaisies littéraires, galantes, politiques et autres d'un grand Seigneur, Le Comte de Lauraguais," *Revue des Etudes Historiques* (Paris: Alphonse Picard, 1914), p. 18. Talma notes regarding the cost that "Lekain only brings it to 20,000 francs in the first edition of his *Mémoires* but it exceeded 60,000 francs. (The author of this note saw the accounts.)" (P. 147, n. 1).

26. Cited by Jullien, *Le Spectateur*, p. 21.

27. Elie Fréron, *L'Année littéraire*, May 3, 1759 (Geneva: Slatkine Reprints, 1966), VI, p. 175, and Collé, *Journal*, II, p. 274. Regarding the personnel involved, Lekain's manuscript *Journal* notes that "The whole executed by Mr. Desboeufs the architect, Mr. Brunetty the painter, Mr. Baucheron the carpenter, Mr. Carton the machinist, at the pleasure of the King" (cited by Olivier, *Le Kain*, p. 170). An additional detail is furnished by a 1759 invoice in the Archives of the Comédie Française: "Statement of what is due Mr. Morguet, master millworker in Paris [for work] carried out at the Comédie Française by order of Mr. Lekain to wit from the 22 March to the 23 ... for ... having worked 2 days and half a night 4 men and the master ... " *(Documents comptables*, carton 14). Unfortunately, very few other *factures* from 1759 have survived.

28. Based on measurements of the Blondel plan, Lagrave *(Public*, pp. 80-81) has concluded that one of the vertical tiers of *balcons* held eight spectators, while the other held ten. My own estimate of the capacity of the new *balcons* derives from a similar interpretation of Benard's "Plan du premier Etage de la Salle de Spectacle de la Comédie Française," which appears in the *Encyclopédie*, (Paris: Briasson, 1772), vol. X, alphabetical page v, within the group of plates titled "Théâtre." I am assuming that the *Encyclopédie* plan shows the theatre essentially as it was in 1759, since it is unlikely that another major remodeling would have taken place soon again, and since no mention of further change is made by contemporary publications. The *Année littéraire* (May 3, 1759, VI, p. 175) notes that "stage boxes were done like at the Opéra, but better designed and more comfortable." According to the Dumont plan of the Opéra the *balcons* there had three benches running the entire width of the box, and a fourth, shorter, bench against the back wall (see fig. 30).

29. Barbier, *Journal*, VII, p. 162. This account of the remodeling is mentioned by Berret, "Comment la scène," p. 457, who further refers the reader to a plan in the Archives of the Comédie Française. To my knowledge, such a plan is not now among the holdings of the Comédie Française. Barbier's figure of 180 is all the more curious in that the same number is given twenty-two years later as the capacity of the *parquet* at the Comédie Italienne.

30. Neither the Dumont plan nor the *Encyclopédie* plan seems to have been created with much care. No scale appears with the Dumont plan which, though labeled "Plan du 1er Etage de la Sale de Spectacle de la Comédie Françoise" (plan at stage-level of the Comédie Française), and clearly representing that theatre, speaks in the legend of "L'Intérieur de la Sale de l'Opera de Paris" (interior of the Paris Opera House). The *Encyclopédie* plan appears to be a copy of the Blondel plan, with the removal of stage benches and orchestra pit improvised without benefit of a site visit.

31.   Roubo, *La Construction*, p. 28. According to Bonnassies, records show that in 1758 the Comédie Française was entitled to twelve musicians, and in 1760 to fourteen. In 1764, this number rose to eighteen, where it remained for some time (*La Musique à la Comédie Française* [Paris: Baur, 1874]).

32.   As described by Bonnassies *(Bâtiments*, p. 19), the *petites loges* were "occupied by important ladies who love the theatre and who attend in casual dress, carrying fans with a peep-hole, to see without being seen, and bring cushions, foot-warmers and even their little dogs."

33.   The language of the lease is excerpted from an unpublished *bail de loge* (Archives Nationales, Minutier Central des Notaires de Paris, XLIV 431, May 19, 1759). Louis-François de Bourbon, Prince de Conti, was a steadfast patron of the arts who probably welcomed the *loges grillées* as a means of attending the Comédie Française in the company of his long-time mistress, the Comtesse de Boufflers.

34.   This number is based on the assumption that the price of a *loge grillée* was calculated on the same basis as that of a *petite loge*. In eleven *bails de loge* I examined (Minutier Central, XLIV 430 and 431, January to May, 1759), one-half of a "petite loge à 4 places," which is to say two seats, was priced at 1,000 *livres* for the year. Applying this figure to the Prince de Conti's lease, 1,250 *livres* per quarter would amount to 5000 *livres* on a yearly basis, or the equivalent of ten seats.

35.   Barbier, VII, *Journal*, p. 163.

36.   Graph of "Recette à l'Entrée, 1680-1793," Alasseur, *Comédie*, p. 48.

37.   The standard measure at the time was the *toise d'ordonnance* which contained six *pieds*, which in turn contained twelve *pouces*. The *toise* was the equivalent of 1.949 meters or 6.394 feet. The *pied* thus equaled 1.065 feet and the *pouce* 1.065 inches. The stage opening, therefore, would have been increased from 15.975 feet (4.875 meters) to 31.95 feet (9.75 meters).

38.   *Mercure de France*, May 1759, p. 187. Further public praise of the Comte de Lauraguais was forthcoming from Voltaire in his dedication to *l'Ecossaise* the following year: "You have rendered an eternal service to Fine Arts and to good taste by your generous gift to the city of Paris of a stage that is not so unworthy of it. If the stage no longer shows Cesar and Ptolomey, Athalie and Joad, Mérope and her son, surrounded and crowded by a flock of young men, if theatre is more appropriate, it is to you alone that this is due." Cited by Peyronnet, *La Mise en scène*, p. 100.

39.   Fromageot, *"Les Fantaisies,"* p. 19.

Chapter 7

1.   Receipts for the closing and opening performances of the preceding seasons were lower, indicating that the public had gone out of its way to purchase the expensive seats for the performances in question. These and all other attendance figures are from Lancaster, *Comédie Française, 1701-1774*.

2.   May 3, 1759, VI, pp. 174-75.

3.   May 1759, p. 186.

4.   *Mercure*, May 1759, p. 187 and *Année litt.*, May 3, 1759, VI, p. 175.

5.   *Journal*, VII, p. 162.

6. May, 1759, pp. 186-87.

7. *Journal*, II, p. 172.

8. May, 1759; cited by Peyronnet, *La Mise en scène*, p. 101.

9. 1760, pp. 53-54.

10. *Année litt.*, VI, p. 175.

11. May 1759, p. 187.

12. *Bâtiments*, p. 22. Bonnassies is doubtless referring to *La Sécchia rapita*, the epi-comic poem by Tassoni (1617), based on a thirteenth-century incident in which the carrying off of a pail from Modena to Bologna precipitated a war.

13. François Charles Gaudet, *Bibliothèque des petits-maitres* (Paris: Lolo, 1762), pp. 84-85. And, some years later, Dorat writes:

    > The public no longer sees, limited in its gaze,
    > Our marquis glittering on triple ramparts.
    > They have ceased embellishing Pharasmane's court,
    > Zaïre has no witness to her conversation with Orosmane.
    > One can no longer observe the ennui of our young nobles
    > Nonchalantly smiling at the heroine in tears.
    > They can no longer be heard from the depths of the wings,
    > Interrupting the actress with their noisy cackle,
    > Mocking Mithridate, and without respect for the name,
    > Abruptly addressing Cesar, or being familiar with Nero.

    This passage from *La Déclamation théâtrale*, 1771, is cited by both Jullien, *Le Spectateur*, p. 29, and Peyronnet, *La Mise en scène*, p. 100.

14. Harny de Guerville, *Le Petit-Maître en province, comédie* (Paris: Vve Duchesne, 1765), sc. 8.

15. Henri Lagrave, "La Comédie Française au XVIIIe siècle ou les contradictions d'un privilège," *Revue d'Histoire du Théâtre*, 1980, pp. 135-37 and Lagrave, *Public*, p. 89.

16. Blondel, *Architecture Française*, II, p. 33.

17. The changes were ordered by M. le Duc d'Aumont, who had replaced the Maréchal de Richelieu as first Gentleman of the King's Bed Chamber, and under whose auspices the Comédie Italienne fell. Put in charge of the work was M. Giraut, Architecte et Ingénieur-Machiniste des Spectacles du Roi *(Mercure de France*, May 1765, pp. 196-200 and Des Boulmiers [Jean Auguste Jullien], *Histoire anecdotique et raisonnée du Théâtre Italien* [Paris: Lacombe, 1769], VII, p. 406.)

18. The hall belonged to a certain Fouré (Clarence D. Brenner, *The Théâtre Italien: Its Repertory, 1716-1793*, University of California Publications in Modern Philology, vol. 63 [Berkeley: Univ. of California Press, 1961], p. 9 and *Mercure de France*, June 1760, p. 233 and October 1760, p. 176).

19. *Spectacles de Paris*, 1761, p. 70. The identical text is to be found in Thomas Simon Gueullette, *Notes et souvenirs sur le théâtre italien au XVIIIe siècle*, ed., J. E. Gueullette, Bibliothèque de la Société des historiens du théâtre, vol. XIII (Paris: Droz, 1938), p. 174.

20. May 1765, p. 197. The remaining citations in this paragraph are from the same place.

21. This drawing is carefully analyzed by Martine de Rougemont, "Deux images d'un théâtre, ou l'Image du Théâtre," *Quaderni di Teatro* (Feb. 1981), pp. 51-66.

22.   These calculations are based on measurement of the 1773 Dumont plan of the Hôtel de
        Bourgogne (fig. 38). In a 1781 report addressed to the Gentilhommes de la Chambre, the
        Comédiens Italiens themselves give the capacity of the *parquet* as 180, exactly the figure used
        by Barbier for the Comédie Française (cited by Lagrave, *Public*, p. 89 and Brenner, *Théâtre
        Italien*, p. 16).

23.   October 10, 1760, VII, pp. 556-57. Both of the eliminated elements were pyramid-shaped
        support structures.

24.   Des Boulmiers, *Histoire anecdotique*, VII, p. 405.

25.   "In the eighteenth century, and until the Revolution, a certain number of performances called
        'capitation performances' were given every year at the Opéra. The box-office receipts were for
        the benefit of the actors of that theatre . . . the sum was divided on a per capita basis, prorated
        according to salary" (F. Pougin, *Dictionnaire historique et pittoresque du théâtre et des arts
        qui s'y rattachent* [Paris: Firmin-Didot, 1885], p. 136). Opéra performers, unlike the actors
        and actresses of the Comédie Française and the Comédie Italienne, were not shareholders in
        the troupe, hence did not regularly share profits, as did members of the other two royal
        theatres. Indeed, after the death of Lully, troupe members had to contend with rapacious
        owners who regarded the Opéra as "a kind of farm," and who "got rich at its expense" (Abbé
        de La Porte et S.R.N. Chamfort, *Dictionnaire dramatique, contenant l'histoire des
        théâtres* . . . [Paris: Lacombe, 1776], II, p. 334.)

26.   The *Mercure de France* reported regularly on these events, for example, April and May 1740
        (pp. 763 and 991) and April 1760, I, p. 197.

27.   "Ordonnance du Roi, Portant Règlement sur les entrées aux Représentations et Répétitions
        de l'Opéra," March 29, 1776, reproduced in Des Essarts, *Les trois théâtres*, p. 289.

28.   Louis Petit de Bachaumont, *Mémoires secrets* (London: Johm Adamsohn, 1786), XXVIII, p.
        217.

29.   April 1765, Slatkine, vol. 68, p. 267.

30.   *Journal de Paris*, December 24, 1778, cited in "Une matinée gratuite à la Comédie Française
        en 1778," *Bulletin de la Société Historique du Théâtre*, 1910, p. 249.

31.   Cited by Babeau, *Le Théâtre des Tuileries*, p. 40.

32.   Bachaumont, *Mémoires secrets*, XXV, pp. 201-2 (March 31, 1784).

33.   See Roselyne La Place, "Des théâtres d'enfants au XVIIIe siècle, *Revue d'Histoire du Théâtre*
        1980, pp. 21-31.

34.   *Année litt.*,V, p. 657.

35.   Information and citations from Karl Mantzuis, *A History of Theatrical Art in Ancient and
        Modern Times*, transl. Louise von Cossel (1904; rpt. Gloucester, Mass: Peter Smith, 1970),
        III, pp. 119-22.

36.   Cited by Leo Hughes, *The Drama's Patrons: A Study of the 18th Century London Audience*
        (Austin: Univ. of Texas Press, 1971), p. 21.

37.   *An Apology for the Life of Mr. Colley Cibber, Written by Himself*, ed. Robert W. Lowe
        (London: John C. Nimmo, 1889), I, p. 234.

38.   Allardyce Nicoll, *The Development of the Theatre*, 5th ed. (London: Harrap, 1966), p. 79.

39.   Johann Wolfgang von Goethe, *The Autobiography of Goethe. Truth and Poetry: From My
        Own Life*, transl. John Oxenford, Esq. (London: Geo. Bell & Sons, 1881), pp. 73-74.

40.   Riccoboni, *Réflexions*, p. 61.

41.   Cited by Jullien, *Le Spectateur*, p. 15.

42.   Ibid.

Chapter 8

1.   T. E. Lawrenson, *The French Stage in the 17th Century* (Manchester: Manchester Univ. Press, 1957), pp. 114-15.

2.   This appraisal, as well as most of the following supporting commentary, is taken from Deierkauf-Holsboer (1960), pp. 55-60.

3.   The *Mémoire de Mahelot* calls for a room with four doors ("chambre à quatre portes") for the *Cid*, each door presumably leading in from one of the four suppressed compartments. This at once created complete unity of place, yet suggested the variety of the *décor multiple* (Lancaster, *History*, II, p. 126 and Lawrenson, *The French Stage*, p. 103).

4.   Lancaster, *History*, II, p. 317.

5.   Lawrenson, *The French Stage*, p. 85.

6.   Vanuxem, "Le Décor," p. 197.

7.   Blondel, *Architecture Française*, II, p. 33.

8.   Peyronnet, *La Mise en scène*, p. 67.

9.   Cited by Peyronnet, *La Mise en scène*, p. 67.

10.   Barnard Hewitt, ed., *The Renaissance Stage, Documents of Serlio, Sabbattini and Furttenbach* (Coral Gables, Fla.: Univ. of Miami Press, 1958), p. 92. This passage in French translation is cited by Villiers, *RHT* 1977, pp. 34-35. Villiers suggests that Sabbattini's warning is directed specifically at the *petits marquis*, a context which does not exist in the original.

11.   Though the relatively simple *Devineresse*, was still performed as late as 1739, complicated spectacles had been removed from the repertory much earlier. The last performance of *Circé*, took place in 1706.

12.   Per Bjurström, "Mises en scène de *Sémiramis* de Voltaire en 1748 et 1759," *Revue d'Histoire du Théâtre*, 1956, p. 299.

13.   Most of the information about stage decoration before and after the removal of the *petits marquis* is taken from Lancaster, *Louis XV*, pp. 439, 475, 509, 545, 615 and 621.

14.   Cited by Lancaster, *Louis XV*, p. 335.

15.   Ibid., p. 303.

16.   Gosta M. Bergman, *Lighting in the Theatre* (Tottowa, N.J.: Rowman & Littlefield, 1977), p. 176.

17.   Cited by Peyronnet, *La Mise en scène*, p. 99, from Lekain's manuscript, "Matériaux pour le travail de mon répertoire tragique."

18.   September 1759, p. 200. When the play was performed the following season, the *Mercure* was even more enthusiatic: "On Saturday the 19th, a performance of *Sémiramis* was given....It seems, since the change in the stage, that it is a different work, so essential is it that good things be properly shown! The scene with the throne, in the third act, and the one with the tomb, in the fifth, make the greatest impression" (May 1760, pp. 182-83).

19. Bjurström. *Sémiramis*, pp. 316-17.

20. Bricaire de la Dixmerie in 1765, cited by Peyronnet, *La Mise en scène*, p. 96. Information about *Iphigénie* is taken from Peyronnet, from Bergman, *Lighting*, p. 162 and from Lancaster, *History*, IV, p. 93.

21. Olivier has made a study of these manuscript notes and the material in this and the next few paragraphs is based on *Le Kain*, pp. 171-72.

22. Cited by Olivier, p. 171, from Lekain's *Etudes manuscrites*.

23. Cited by Lancaster, *Louis XV*, p. 127.

24. The *Mercure* for May 1759 offers a description: "In the first act of *Brutus*, for example, in order to shift from the Capitol to the house of the Consuls, no change was made other than the removal of an altar from the middle of the stage" (p. 186).

25. Bergman, *Lighting*, p. 176.

26. In a letter to his niece, Mme de Fontaine, dated May 5, 1759, he writes: "You advise me, in the meantime, to do a tragedy, because the stage is purged of *petits-maîtres*. I, do a tragedy, after what the great Jean-Jacques has written against theatre! Look out for the eyes in your head if you ever say that I am the kind of man to do a tragedy. No indeed, I do not do tragedy ... " (cited by Jullien, *Le Spectateur*, p. 26).

27. Passages from Voltaire cited by Jullien, *Le Spectateur*, pp. 26 and 27.

28. Peyronnet, *La Mise en scène*, p. 103.

29. Lancaster, *Louis XV*, pp. 414 and 416.

30. Cited by Lancaster, *Louis XV*, p. 516.

31. Cited by Olivier, *Le Kain*, p. 171, from Bachaumont's *Mémoires secrets*.

32. Peyronnet, *La Mise en scène*, p. 103.

33. Cited by Lancaster, *Louis XV*, p. 545.

34. After more than 80 years, the theatre on the rue des Fossés-Saint-Germain-des-Prés was in a state of decrepitude. While awaiting construction of their new theatre to be located at Place de l'Odéon, the troupe occupied the former Salle des Machines. Neither the stage nor the auditorium of this vast theatre was suitable to performance of tragedy and comedy, but the *comédiens* were obliged to put up with this arrangement until 1882, when the Odéon Theatre was completed. (Sylvie Chevalley, *La Comédie-Française hier et aujourd'hui* [Paris: Didier, 1979], pp. 24-25.)

35. Lancaster, *Louis XV*, p. 621.

36. Peyronnet, *La Mise en scène*, p. 105.

37. Cited by Peyronnet, *La Mise en scène*, p. 97.

38. Not in a hurry, the *Mercure* did not get around to this item until February of 1696, some seven years after the opening of the new theatre. Cited by Pierre Mélèse, "Les Conditions materielles du Théâtre à Paris sous Louis XIV," *Dix-Septième Siècle* (1958), No. 39, p. 108.

39. Information about candles is based upon Bergman's transcription of a portion of the 1719 record kept by the Comédie Française entitled *Depense des chandelles ordinaires...* (Bergman, *Lighting*, p. 155).

40. May 3, 1759, VI, p. 175.

41. Footlight and wing lighting information is from Olivier, *Le Kain*, p. 172 and Bergman, *Lighting*, pp. 170-71.

Bibliography

Manuscripts

Archives of the Comédie Française. "Dépenses de l'Etablissement par Monsieur de la Grange—20 juin 1687 au 17 novembre 1691." Carton 171.

_____. Invoices, receipts and related documents. Cartons 14 and 151 and the 1715 folder.

_____. Feuilles d'assemblée des Comédiens Français.

_____. Registres journaliers, 1673–1680.

_____. Registres journaliers, 1680–1774. (Also on microfilm at the Library of Congress. MLA deposit, 523 F, 561 F, 808 F.)

Archives Nationales. Minutier Central des Notaires de Paris. VI, 589 and XLIV 431.

_____. Service des plans, cartes et dessins. O' 3238 fol. 32.

Bibiliothèque Historique de la Ville de Paris. Various ordinances in 138 450 and N.F. 35 380.

Bibliothèque Nationale. Cabinet des Estampes. Ed 42a, 0a 58 fol. 15–24, 0a 78 pet. fol., 0a 79 pet. fol., Va 263, t. 1.

_____. Salle des Manuscrits, ff9236 and Fonds de la Mare, ff21625.

_____. Réserve, G.F. 15 (217) 1698.

Bibliothèque de l'Opéra. Registres journaliers de l'Opéra Comique, 1717–1825. (Also on microfilm at the Library of Congress, MLA deposit.)

Printed Works

Aghion, Max. Le Théâtre à Paris au XVIIIe siècle. Paris: Lib. de France, 1926.

Alasseur, Claude. La Comédie Française au 18e siècle: étude économique. Paris: Mouton, 1967.

Aubignac, L'Abbé d'. La pratique du théâtre. Ed. P. Martino. Paris: Champion, 1927.

Babeau, Albert. Le Théâtre des Tuileries sous Louis XIV, Louis XV et Louis XVI. Nogent-le-Rotrou: Daupeley-Gouverneur, 1895.

Bachaumont, Louis Petit de. Mémoires secrets. 36 vols. London: Johm Adamsohn, 1777–1789.

Bapst, Germain. Essai sur l'histoire du théâtre, la mise en scène, le décor, le costume, l'architecture, l'éclairage, l'hygiène. Paris: Lahure, 1893.

Barbier, Edmond-Jean-François. Chronique de la Régence et du règne de Louis XV (1718–1763) or Journal de Barbier. Paris: Charpentier, 1857. Vol. VII.

Barlow, Graham. "The Hôtel de Bourgogne According to Sir James Thornhill." Theatre Research International, I, No. 2 (1976), pp. 86–98.

Bergman, Gosta M. Lighting in the Theatre. Tottowa, N.J.: Rowman & Littlefield, 1977.

Berret, P. "Comment la scène française du XVIIIe siècle a été débarassée de la présence des gentilshommes." Revue d'hostoire littéraire, 1901, pp. 456–59.

Bjurström, Per. "Mises en scène de Sémiramis de Voltaire en 1748 et 1759." Revue d'Histoire du Théâtre, vol. 8 (1956), pp. 299–320.

Blondel, Jacques-François. *Architecture Française*, 4 vols. Paris: C. A. Jombert, 1752–1756.

Bonnassies, Jules. *La Comédie Française. Histoire administrative, 1658–1757*. Paris: Didier, 1874.

———. *La Comédie Française. Notice historique sur les anciens bâtiments*. Paris: Aubry, 1868.

———. *La Musique à la Comédie Française*. Paris: Baur, 1874.

Bourdel, Nicole. "L'établissement et la construction de l'Hôtel des Comédiens Français, rue des Fossés-Saint-Germain-des-Prés (Ancienne Comédie) 1687–90." *Revue d'Histoire du Théâtre*, vol. 7 (1955), pp. 145–72.

Boursault. *Les Fables d'Esope*. Paris: T. Girard, 1690.

Brenner, Clarence D. *A Bibliographical List of Plays in the French Language, 1700–1789*. Berkeley, California, 1947.

———. *The Théâtre Italien: Its Repertory, 1716–1793*. University of California Publications in Modern Philology, vol. 63. Berkeley: Univ. of California Press, 1961.

Brillon, Pierre-Jacques. *Le Théophraste moderne, ou Nouveaux caractères des moeurs*. Paris: Brunet, 1701.

Castex, Surer and Becker. *Manuel des études littéraires françaises, XVIIe siècle*. Paris: Hachette, 1966.

Chappuzeau, Samuel. *Le Théâtre Français, divisé en trois livres, où il est traité de l'usage de la Comédie, des auteurs qui soutiennent le théâtre, de la conduite des comédiens*. Paris: 1674; rpt. Paris: J. Bonnassies, 1876.

Chassaigne, Marc. *La Lieutenance générale de police de Paris*. 1906; rpt. Geneva: Slatkine-Megariotis, 1975.

Chevalley, Sylvie, ed. *Registre d'Hubert. Revue d'Histoire du Théâtre*, 1973, nos. 1 and 2.

———. *Registre de La Grange, 1659–1685*. Genève: Minkoff, 1972.

———. *La Comédie-Française hier et aujourd'hui*. Paris: Didier, 1979.

Cianorescu, Alexandre. "Baroque et action dramatique: le dehors et le dedans," in *Le Baroque au théâtre et la théâtralité du Baroque*. Montauban: CNRS, 1967.

Cibber, Colley. *An Apology for the Life of Mr. Colley Cibber*, Written by Himself. Ed. Robert W. Lowe. London: John C. Nimmo, 1889. Vol. I.

Clément, Jean-Marie-Bernard and de la Porte, Abbé Jean-Barthélemy. *Anecdotes dramatiques*. Paris: Vve Duchesne, 1775.

Clinton-Baddely, V.C. *All-Right in the Night*. London: Putnam, 1954.

Cohen, Gustave. *L'Evolution dans la mise en scène dans le théâtre français*. Lille: Lefebvre-Ducrocq, 1910.

Collé, Charles. *Journal et mémoires*. Ed..H. Bonhomme. 3 vols. Paris: Didot, 1868.

Curtis, A. Ross. "A Propos d'une gravure de 1662." *Revue d'Histoire du Théâtre*, 1967, pp. 97–98.

De Belloy, Pierre Laurent. *Oeuvres complètes*. Paris: Moutard, 1779. Vol. I.

Decugis, Nicole and Reymond, Suzanne. *Le Décor de théâtre en France du Moyen Age à 1925*. Paris: Cie française des arts graphiques, 1953.

Deierkauf-Holsboer, S. Wilma. *Histoire de la mise en scène dans le Théâtre Français de 1600 à 1657*. Bibliothèque de la Société des Historiens du Théâtre, I. Paris: Droz, 1933.

———. *Histoire de la mise en scène dans le Théâtre Français, à Paris, de 1600 à 1673*. Paris: Nizet, 1960.

———. *Le Théâtre de l'Hôtel de Bourgogne*. 2 vols. Paris: Nizet, 1968–70.

———. *Le Théâtre du Marais*, 2 vols. Paris: Nizet 1954–58.

Deloffre, Frédéric, ed. Marivaux, *Petit-maître corrigé*. Geneva: Droz, 1955.

Des Boulmiers (Jean Auguste Jullien). *Histoire anecdotique et raisonnée du Théâtre Italien*. Paris: Lacombe, 1769. Vol. VII.

Descotes, Maurice. *Le public de théâtre et son histoire*. Paris: P.U.F., 1964.

Des Essarts, dit Nicolas-Toussaint le Moyne. *Les trois théâtres de Paris, ou Abrégé historique de l'établissement de la Comédie Française, de la Comédie Italienne et de l'Opéra*. Paris: Lacombe, 1777.

Des Lauriers (Bruscambille). *Les Fantaisies de Bruscambille*. Paris: F. Lambert, 1668.
Despois, Eugène. *Le Théâtre français sous Louis XIV*. Paris: Hachette, 1874.
Diderot, Denis. *Correspondance*. Ed. Georges Roth. Paris: Editions de Minuit, 1956. Vol. II, pp. 89–90 (November 27, 1758).
———. *Le Père de famille*, in *Oeuvres complètes*, eds., J. Assézat and M. Tourneaux, vol. VII. Paris: Garnier, 1875.
Dubech, Lucien. *Histoire générale illustrée du théâtre*. Paris: Librairie de France, 1932. Vol. II.
Dubois, Claude-Gilbert. *Le Baroque: profondeurs de l'apparence*. Paris: Librairie Larousse, 1973.
Dumont, Gabriel-Martin. *Parallèle des plans des plus belles salles de spectacles d'Italie et de France*. Paris: 1774; rpt. New York: B. Blom, 1968.
Du Tralage, Jean Nicolas. *Mélanges sur la Comédie et l'Opéra, extraits du manuscript de Jean Nicolas du Tralage*, in *Notes et documents sur l'histoire des théâtres de Paris*. Ed. Jacob. Paris: Librairie des bibliophiles, P. Lacroix, 1880.
Encyclopédie. Paris: Briasson, 1772.
Ford, Franklin L. *Robe and Sword: The Regrouping of the French Aristocracy after Louis XIV*. New York: Harper and Row, 1953.
Fournel, Victor. *Curiosités théâtrales anciennes et modernes françaises et étrangères*. Paris: Delahays, 1859.
Franklin, Alfred. *La Vie privée d'autrefois: arts, et métiers, modes, moeurs, usages des Parisiens, du XIIe au XVIIIe siècle*. Paris: Plon et Nourrit, 1898. Vol. XXI.
Fréron, Elie. *L'Année littéraire, 1754–1791*. Vols. V–VII. Geneva: Slatkine Reprints, 1966.
Fritsche, Hermann. "La Scène de Molière et son organisation." *Le Moliériste*, June 1887. No. 99, pp. 65–77.
Fromageot, P. "Les Fantaisies littéraires, galantes, politiques et autres d'un grand Seigneur. Le Comte de Lauraguais." *Revue des Etudes Historiques*. Paris: Alphonse Picard, 1914.
Furetière, Antoine. *Dictionnaire Universel*. 3 vols. 1690; Geneva: Slatkine Reprints, 1970.
Gaudet, François Charles. *Bibliothèque des petits-maîtres*. Paris: Lolo, 1762.
Goethe, Johann Wolfgang von. *The Autobiography of Goethe. Truth and Poetry: From My Own Life*. Transl. John Oxenford, Esq. London: Geo. Bell & Sons, 1881.
Gossip, C. J. "Le Décor de théâtre au collège des Jésuites à Paris au XVIIe siècle." *Revue d'Histoire du Théâtre* (1981), pp. 26–38.
Grimm, Friedrich-Melchior, et al. *Correspondance littéraire, philosophique et critique*. Ed. M. Tourneaux. 16 vols. Paris: Garnier, 1877–1882.
Gueullette, Thomas Simon. *Notes et souvenirs sur le théâtre italien au XVIIIe siècle*. Ed. J.E. Gueullette. Bibliothèque de la Société des historiens du théâtre, vol. XIII. Paris: Droz, 1938.
Guibert, Noëlle. "La Place du décor dans le théâtre du XVIIe siècle en France." *Comédie Française*, no. 94 (1980), 33–37.
Harny de Guerville. *Le Petit-Maître en province, comédie*. Paris: Vve Duchesne, 1765.
Hewitt, Barnard, ed. *The Renaissance Stage, Documents of Serlio, Sabbattini and Furttenbach*. Coral Gables, Fla.: Univ. of Miami Press, 1958.
Histoire des Spectacles, ed. Guy Dumur. Encyclopédia de la Pléiade. Paris: N.R.F., 1965.
Hughes, Leo. *The Drama's Patrons: A Study of the 18th Century London Audience*. Austin: Univ. of Texas Press, 1971.
Huss, William. "La Troupe de l'Hôtel Guénégaud, 1677–1680." Diss., Univ. of Paris X, 1978.
Illingworth, David V. "Documents inédits et nouvelles précisions sur le Théâtre de l'Hôtel de Bourgogne d'apres des documents du dix-huitième siècle." *Revue d'Histoire du Théâtre*, 1970, pp. 125–32.
Jullien, Adolphe. *Le Spectateur sur la scène*. Paris: Detaille, 1875.
Jürgens, Madeleine and Maxfield-Miller, Elizabeth. *Cent ans de recherches sur Molière*. Paris: Imp. Nationale, 1963.

Lagrave, Henri. "La Comédie Française au XVIIIe siècle ou les contradictions d'un privilège." *Revue d'Histoire du Théâtre*, 1980, pp. 127–41.

_____. *Le Théâtre et la public à Paris de 1715 à 1750*. Paris: Klincksieck, 1972.

Lancaster, Henry Carrington. *The Comédie Française, 1680–1701: Plays, Actors, Spectators, Finances*, Johns Hopkins Studies in Romance Literatures and Languages, ex. vol. 17. Baltimore: The Johns Hopkins Press, 1941.

_____. *The Comédie Française, 1701–1774*, Transactions of the American Philosophical Society, N. S. vol. 41, part 4. Philadelphia: Am. Phil. Soc., 1951.

_____. *French Tragedy in the Time of Louis XV and Voltaire, 1715–1774*. Baltimore: Johns Hopkins Press, 1950.

_____. *A History of French Dramatic Literature in the Seventeenth Century*. 9 vols. Baltimore: Johns Hopkins Press, 1929–42.

_____. *Sunset, A History of Parisian Drama in the Last Years of Louis XIV, 1701–1715*. Baltimore: Johns Hopkins Press, 1945.

La Place, Roselyne. "Des théâtres d'enfants au XVIIIe siècle." *Revue d'Histoire du Théâtre*, 1980, pp. 21–31.

La Porte, Abbé de and Chamfort, S.R.N. *Dictionnaire dramatique contenant l'histoire des théâtres....* Paris: Lacombe, 1776. Vol. II.

Lawrenson, T. E. *The French Stage in the 17th Century*. Manchester: MUP, 1957.

_____. "The Shape of the 18th Century French Theatre and the Drawing Board Renaissance." *Recherches Théâtrales*, vol. VII, nos. 1–3 (1966).

_____. and Purkis, Helen. "Les Editions illustrées de Térence dans l'histoire du théâtre: spectacles dans un fauteuil?," in *Le Lieu théâtral à la Renaissance*, ed. Jean Jacquot. Paris: Editions du Centre national de la recherche scientifique, 1968, pp. 1–24.

Leclerc, Ludovic (Celler). *Les Décors, les costumes et la mise en scène au XVIIe siècle (1615–1680)*. 1869; rpt. Geneva: Slatkine, 1970.

Lekain, Henri Louis Cain. Ed. Talma. *Mémoires de Lekain, précédés de réflexions sur cet acteur, et sur l'art théâtral*. Paris: 1825; rpt. Geneva: Slatkine, 1968.

Lemazurier, Pierre-David. *Galérie historique des acteurs du Théâtre français, depuis 1600 jusqu'à nos jours*. 2 vols. Paris: Chaumerot, 1810.

Léris, Antoine de. *Dictionnaire portatif historique et littéraire des théâtres*. Paris: 1763; rpt. Geneva: Slatkine, 1970.

Lough, John. *Paris Theatre Audiences in the 17th and 18th Centuries*. London: Oxford Univ. Press, 1957.

_____. "A Paris Theatre in the Eighteenth Century." *University of Toronto Quarterly*, 1958, pp. 289–304.

_____. *Seventeenth-Century French Drama: the Background*. Oxford: Clarendon Press, 1979.

Luynes, Duc de. *Mémoires sur la Cour de Louis XV, 1735–1738*. Paris: Firmin-Didot, 1860–1865. Vol. XI.

Lyonnet, Henry. *Les Premières de Pierre Corneille*. Paris: Delagrave, 1923.

Mantzuis, Karl. *A History of Theatrical Art in Ancient and Modern Times*. Transl. Louise von Cossel. 1904; rpt. Gloucester, Mass.: Peter Smith, 1970. Vol. III.

Marmontel, Jean François. *Mémoires*. Ed. M. Tourneux. Paris: Librairie des Bibliophiles, 1891.

Melèse, Pierre. "Les Conditions materielles du Théâtre à Paris sous Louis XIV." *Dix-Septième Siècle*, no. 39 (1958), pp. 104–24.

_____. *Le Théâtre et le public à Paris sous Louis XIV (1639–1713)*. Paris: Droz, 1934.

Le Mercure, 1721–1723.

Le Mercure de France, 1724–1791.

Mittman, Barbara G. "Cinq documents portant sur l'enceinte de la balustrade à l'Ancienne Comédie." *Revue d'Histoire du Théâtre* (1983), pp. 174–89.

_____. "Les Spectateurs sur la scène: quelques chiffres tirés des registres du XVIIe siècle." *Revue d'Histoire du Théâtre* (1980), pp. 199–215.

Mongrédien, Georges. *Les Grands comédiens au XVIIe siècle.* Paris: Le Livre, 1927.

_____. "Les théâtres en France sous le règne de Louis XIII." In *Il teatro al tempo de Luigi XIII.* Paris: Nizet, 1974.

Monval, Georges, ed. *Le Premier Registre de la Thorillière (1663–64).* Paris: Librairie des Bibliophiles, 1890.

Mouhy, Charles de Fieux, chevalier de. *Abrégé de l'histoire du Théâtre Français depuis son origine jusqu'au premier juin 1780.* Paris: L. Jorry, 1780–1783.

Nagler, A. M. *A Source Book in Theatrical History.* New York: Dover, 1959.

Nicoll, Allardyce. *The Development of the Theatre.* 5th ed. London: Harrap, 1966.

Olivier, Jean-Jacques. *Henri-Louis Le Kain de la Comédie-Française (1729–1778).* Paris: Soc. française d'Imprimerie et de Librairie, 1907.

Origny, A.J.-B.d' *Annales du Théâtre Italien depuis son origine jusqu'à ce jour.* Paris: Vve Duchesne, 1768. Vol. I.

Parfaict, François and Claude. *Histoire du Théâtre Française depuis son origine jusqu'à présent.* 15 vols. Amsterdam: 1735–1749.

Perrault, Charles. *Le Cabinet des beaux-arts.* Paris: G. Edelinck, 1690.

Peyronnet, Pierre. *La Mise en scène au XVIIIe siècle.* Paris: Nizet, 1974.

Poisson, Raymond. *Le Baron de la Crasse* and *Le Zig-Zag.* Paris: G. Quinet, 1662.

Pougin, F. *Dictionnaire historique et pittoresque du théâtre et des arts qui s'y rattachent.* Paris: Firmin-Didot, 1885.

Pure, Michel de. *Idée des spectacles anciens et nouveaux.* Paris: Brunet, 1668.

Rapports inédits du Lieutenant de police René Argenson. 1697–1715. Ed. Paul Cottin. Bibliothèque Elzévirienne. Paris: E. Plon, Nouritt et Cie, 1891.

Riccoboni, Luigi. *Réflexions historiques et critiques sur les différents théâtres de l'Europe.* Paris: J. Guérin, 1738.

Roubo, André Jacob. *Traité de la construction des théâtres et des machines théâtrales.* Paris: Cellot et Jombert, 1777.

Rougemont, Martine de. "Deux images d'un théâtre, ou l'image du Théâtre." *Quaderni di Teatro* (Feb. 1981), pp. 51-66.

Roy, D. H. "La Scène de l'Hôtel de Bourgogne." *Revue d'Histoire du Théâtre,* 1962, pp. 227–35.

Schaffer, Pierre. "Un Théâtre parisien sous Louis XIV: l'Hôtel Guénégaud de 1673 à 1677." Diss., Univ. of Paris X, 1979.

Schwartz, W. L. "Light on Molière in 1664 from 'Le Second Registre de La Thorillière.'" PMLA, LIII (1938), pp. 1054-75.

_____. "Molière's Theatre in 1672–1673: Light from Le Registre d'Hubert." PMLA, LVI (1941), pp. 395–427.

Sennett, Richard. *The Fall of the Public Man.* New York: Vintage Books–Random House, 1978.

Shaffer, Peter. *Equus.* New York: Samuel French, 1973.

Les Spectacles de Paris, ou suite du Calendrier historique et chronologique des théâtres. Paris: Duchesne, 1754–1794.

Tallemant des Réaux. *Les Histoirettes.* Ed. G. Mongrédien. Paris: Garnier, 1934. Vol. VII.

Tidworth, Simon. *Theatres: an Illustrated History.* London: Pall Mall Press, 1973.

"Une matinée gratuite à la Comédie Française en 1778." *Bulletin de la Société Historique du Théâtre,* 1910, p. 249.

Vanuxem, Jacques. "Le Décor de théâtre sous Louis XIV." *Dix-Septième Siècle,* no. 39 (1958), 196-217.

Villiers, André. "L'Ouverture de la scène à l'Hôtel de Bourgogne." *Revue d'Histoire du Théâtre,* 1970, pp. 133–41.

_____. "Sur la pratique du rideau de scène au XVIIème siècle." *Revue d'Histoire du Théâtre*, 1977, pp. 30-40.

Voltaire. *Oeuvres complètes*. Ed. L. Moland. Paris: Garnier, 1883-1885. 52 volumes (vols. 2-7).

_____. *Correspondence*. Ed. T. Besterman. Geneva: Institut et Musée Voltaire, 1953-1965. 107 volumes.

Wiley, William L. *The Early Public Theatre in France*. Cambridge, Mass.: Harvard Univ. Press, 1960.

_____. *The Hôtel de Bourgogne. Another Look at France's First Public Theatre*. Studies in Philology, vol. LXX, no. 5. Chapel Hill: Univ. of North Carolina Press, 1973.

Young, Bert Edward and Young, Grace Philputt, eds. *Le Registre de La Grange, 1659–1685*. Paris: Droz, 1947.

Index